I miss ,
I hope
the stories. Thank you
Lovingly

Double Entry

Helen Gray Christopher

Helen Gray Christopher

2/8/97

DEDICATION

$\mathcal{T}$o my mother and father who were responsible for Bill's and my double entry.

To my husband, Ian, who was patient while I wrote these reminiscences and tactfully suggested, without results, that I put in asterisks and add foot notes such as: This is where my husband ran out of socks.

To our children, James Gray, Sonja Lee, Gretchen Diane, and William Ian (in chronological order) and Jim's wife, Gina. They all shared time, energy and ideas which helped me stay aboard when increasing responsibilities and junk mail threatened to swamp the boat.

To Bill, my twin, who speaks for himself in the following pages.

THE TWINS:
WILLIAM PRICE GRAY, JR. AND HELEN GRAY CHRISTOPHER (1954)

OLYMPIA LITTLE THEATER CO-FOUNDER HELEN CHRISTOPHER (MRS. IAN)
IN MAKEUP AS MELISSA IN *ONE FINE DAY*, OLT'S FIRST PRODUCTION, 1939.
PHOTO BY JAMES STANFORD.

FOREWORD

These memoirs, begun nearly forty-eight years ago, were written to picture for my children and grandchildren what it was like when William and I, "the Gray Twins," were growing up in the small town of Wilbur, Washington. That town, together with remarkable parents, provided William and me with colorful examples of people, baseball, school, politics, business, theatrics—you name it!

Both the happy and the difficult experiences, made lasting impressions on both of us...they provided William and me with examples of helping others, of ethical behavior and community service worthy of emulation. For us they helped shape our lives and influenced what we became as adults.

Because of a troublesome back, by the late forties I could no longer enjoy the fulfillment gained from acting or directing of OLT (Olympia Little Theater) plays. A founder in 1939, I now needed a replacement to fill that void.

The answer came as Ian and I were returning from a performance in Tacoma. Something triggered memories of happenings that needed to be written. *Double Entry* was begun. Perfect—I wrote in the middle of the night or anytime for about two years, not always these recollections, but I was writing. Then gradually community projects began to crowd that out. Writing was confined to such things as Letters to the Editor, Scripts for Slide Shows, Histories of OLT and ASCM (Associates of the State Capitol Museum) and finally a stab at Short Story writing.

We moved to Panorama City in 1992. I enrolled in a writing class there and rediscovered the joys of disciplining oneself to produce. But not until the class ended was working on this autobiographical project begun again.

To have it finished by Christmas 1993 proved an unrealistic goal. Then, in 1995, head overruled heart; I gave up Panorama City Chorus, under Paul Bellam's peerless conducting. Other Panorama activities with interesting friends were put on hold.

But it was my busy, caring neighbor and friend, Jessie Kinnear Kenton, who became my computer teacher, and my daughter, Gretchen, whose hours of work on this project are beyond counting, who kept me going during these last two years. Because of their patience and enthusiasm, these memories are in your hands.

Have fun reading them!
I had fun remembering.

Helen Christopher

PHOTO BY JERRIE BALLEW, AUGUST 1995

CONTENTS

1 WILBUR

5 MAINLY ABOUT MAMA

9 MAINLY ABOUT PAPA

16 MISS GREEN BECOMES MRS. GRAY

18 ABOUT BUSINESS

23 DOUBLE ENTRY

29 THE TWINS

32 MAIN STREET AND BEYOND

36 FIRE!

38 THE BASEBALL LEGEND

42 MEMORIES, GOOD OR BAD

51 MORE ABOUT BUSINESS

61 MORE MEMORIES

66 LESSONS LEARNED

69 LIFE WITH MAMA AND PAPA, CONTINUED

73 CHALLENGES

75 THE PERFORMING ARTS

83 PAPA AND POLITICS

85 FAREWELL TO WILBUR HIGH SCHOOL

89 COLLEGE

98 THE REAL WORLD

106 MARRIAGES

110 PAPA AND POLITICS, CONTINUED

119 MAINLY ABOUT WILLIAM

122 TRANSITIONS

Wilbur

The town where Mama and Papa met, fell in love, married and raised their family was named Wilbur, after the middle name of man known as "Wild Goose Bill" who founded it in 1887.

Almost twenty years earlier, Samuel Wilbur Condit (Condon) had come to the northwest from the gold country of California. While following an Indian trail on one of his freighting and packing jobs from Walla Walla to the Columbia River, he had discovered a fine creek running through a natural meadow land.

The sheltered valley lay between basalt cliffs. The clear waters of Little Ridge (later Goose Creek) were fringed with aspen, cottonwood and willow trees. It was while standing on the north cliff that he determined to make that his home when he was ready to settle down.

On October 27, 1885, the United States Government deeded to Samuel Wilbur Condit eighty acres of land for a total cost of $100. The deed was filed with the Lincoln County Abstract Company at Lincoln County, Washington Territory.

Condit was nicknamed "Wild Goose Bill"—some said because he shot an early settler's barnyard fowl, presumably by mistake. That so infuriated the owner, who had brought the eggs from Oregon, that she chased Condit all the way to his home, while delivering a tirade against the stupidity of a man who pretended to be a frontiersman and didn't know the difference between a tame goose and a wild one.

A second story claimed that the proprietor of the Seventy Mile

1

House Tavern had tamed a brood of wild geese—a fact everyone was aware of. Bill, however, feeling somewhat reckless and a bit hungry for goose, pretended to think the geese were wild. Drawing his revolver, he began picking them off.

Hearing the shooting, the proprietor looked out to see what was going on and, taking in the situation at a glance, rushed out toward the slayer of his fowl, shouting, "Them's my geese! Them's my geese!"

Without looking around, Bill purportedly proceeded to pick off another, while cautioning the owner to "keep still or I'll get the whole flock." And so "Wild Goose Bill" he became, and the label stuck. In formally naming the town, its inhabitants chose the more dignified middle name of its founder, and thus Goosetown became Wilbur on the maps of the young state.

Wilbur's founder had two spellings for his last name. One explanation for the changing of "Condit" to "Condon" was that the Chinese miners and laborers couldn't pronounce "Condit". After they helped complete the building of one of his roads, they traveled to Walla Walla to record the ownership for him, and they told the Government clerk that the owner's name was "Condon." When Bill discovered the error, it was too far for him to travel to change it, so it remained "Condon."

Before getting title to the land, Wild Goose Bill had staked his claim and pitched his tent. He then built a two-story cabin and established a horse and cattle ranch. After acquiring the deed, he opened a post office in 1885, but closed it in 1886.

One chronicler wrote:

"But raising stock was not enough for Bill. He opened a trading post in his home, with a blacksmith shop along side. Considerable traffic passed by his post, heading west to the mining areas in western Canada. In 1872, the Colville Indian Reservation had been established, so much of Condon's trade was with the Indians who lived there, as well as with the Chinese miners and early settlers making their way through the area. This was Wilbur's first business.

"He was a prospector and miner, a packer and freighter, a rancher, a storekeeper, and a ferry man. He built roads and ferries and bridges. He dealt in real estate; he founded a town."

Wilbur's first homes and businesses lay in the flat meadow land between the two bluffs. Near the main street, Goose Creek normally bubbled its way over smooth stones and water plants. Occasionally, however, melting snows from the surrounding hills turned the creek into a muddy river that flooded that part of town.

To handle his real estate, Wild Goose Bill—while busy most of the time with stock raising and operation of his ferry across the Columbia River—hired Wilbur attorney Rollin Joseph Reeves as his agent.

Mr. Reeves was granted (take a deep breath...)

"Irrevocable Power of Attorney for five years to sell and dispose of the lands and by contract to convey for any price not less than hereinafter stated, but said second party shall not sell to any one purchaser more than 24 lots unless 1st party shall join in execution of the deed and make good and sufficient deeds therefor and acknowledge the same."

(I can just see Wild Goose Bill at Lawyer Reeves' elbow, dictating every stipulation—non stop, with little time for punctuation.)

"Party of the second part shall not sell lots in the original town of Wilbur until first party join in execution of the deed and Party of the second part shall not...etc... etc...until first party receives a good and sufficient title deed therefore from the Northern Pacific Company."

(Whew!) By 1899, *a good and sufficient title deed* had been received by Wild Goose Bill, and the town was platted. In August, before two witnesses and notarized by Mr. E. F. Benson *"for and in Washington*

Territory," Samuel Wilbur Condon deeded the Railroad Addition to the town of Wilbur.

The Addition lay south of downtown. (That was where, fourteen years later, Mama and Papa would buy three lots with the two-story three bedroom house that became the family home.)

Like many settlers of his day, Wild Goose Bill loved feverish activity and preferred to die—if die he must—with his boots on.

The wish was granted when shooting it out with another settler— over a woman who had left his bed for that of another man. Samuel Wilbur Condon lost his life near the town that was to bear his middle name.

Gradually wheat farming supplanted stock raising, as pioneers of the Big Bend realized what a rich wheat country they had chosen for their homes.

Mainly About Mama

Mama, named Della Wray Green, was born to Mary Jane Weaver Green and William Alfred Green in Pickering, Nodaway County, Missouri, September 14, 1873. She was the oldest girl among the six boys and four girls. Her sturdy farmer father and hard-working mother were inured to the cyclones and hard times that came to farmers of that section. To supplement the family income, her father, Grandpa Green, did carpentry work, but those earnings were stretched beyond his ability to supply even meager accommodations for the family. Her mother, Grandma Green, as was the custom among neighbors, traded molasses for potatoes and other foodstuffs to give variety to the diet of her family.

There was a cyclone cellar behind the house. As a youngster, Mama early developed a sense of responsibility while helping herd the younger sisters and brothers to safety. There were times when cattle were lifted bodily by swirling funnels of dust and wind, to be carried miles away. Responsibility was an integral part of Mama's character always.

Mama loved the farm but was conscious, nevertheless, of the hardships that her mother endured. As a little girl Mama expressed her ambitions to a family visitor by saying, "When I grow up I want to be a teacher and earn a churn full of money to give to my mama."

She loved school, was a quick and conscientious student. When she had completed the necessary high school requirements three years early, her English instructor took her to the county seat of Marysville, Missouri, to take the teachers' examinations. There, while working for her room and board, she attended summer classes in order to pass the exams and earn the coveted certificate which would make her a fully accredited teacher.

In the late 1800's, the I. H. Brown Common School Examiner and Review had to be mastered by those seeking certification as teachers. The book had over sixty questions and more than two hundred and seventy-five lengthy answers to memorize. I doubt that I could have made it. Mama did at age fifteen.

After the examination one of the examiners said, "I don't know whether we can certificate you or not; you're so young."

Mama's heart sank, but she only asked, "Didn't I do well enough in my examinations?"

The examiner nodded his white-maned head. "Well, yes," he said, "You're right at the top." Then he smiled at her. "I guess we'll just have to give you that diploma, young lady, and just hope that some school board will think you're old enough to teach."

Immediately thereafter, Mama appeared before the Nodaway Country School Board and applied for a position to teach near her home.

"Law, child, you're not as big or as old as some of the boys you'd have," one Board member told her. "Discipline could be a problem."

"Just let me try," she begged.

They did. She succeeded. She was a *natural,* and Mama was rehired for the next school term and for as many more as she wanted to continue in that school.

ॐ

Seventy years later, after Mama's death in 1957, her brother Don, next to the youngest of her siblings, wrote me:

> "When your Aunt Faye was born I was sent to the kitchen which had recently been added to with money furnished by your mother. Before that we were nine children in only three rooms.
>
> "Also we had a new smoke house, they called it. More properly it was a store room separate from the house, with a

toilet, which we had never had 'til this time. The money for the lumber had been furnished by your mother.

"We never had a well until I was about six years old. I don't know whether your mother paid for the drilling or not, but I suspect she did.

"She taught school about three miles from where we lived, and I went to school to her the first two years. She had a gray mare named Daisy and a two-wheeled cart—no cover. The older boys hitched up Daisy and brought her to the gate; we got in and went to school. The older boys at school unhitched her and hitched her again when school was out. When it got real cold and snowy we would stay at some people's that lived a short distance from the school. The name of that school was Sunrise. That was the last two years before she went to Wilbur.

"I remember when your mother wore a sailor hat, and leg of mutton sleeves, used Ayres Hair Tonic, and brushed her hair a hundred times a day. It came to her waist."

After Mama had saved money enough to buy an organ for the family and a sewing machine for her sister Jessie who was clever with the needle, the young school teacher came west in 1896 to visit her brother Earl. He was working in the state of Washington. At that time she took out a homestead claim near the present Grand Coulee Dam.

Mama came in the spring since the Missouri schools kept for only six months out of each year. Then in order to replenish her purse before returning to Missouri in the late fall, she accepted a position as teacher during June and July in a little country school in the Grand Coulee country which couldn't afford a full term teacher in the winter. There, as in Missouri, her transportation was by horse.

Mama was a frequent visitor to the town of Wilbur, which was the largest town anywhere near her boarding place. In the M. E. & E. T. Hay Department Store, Mama opened a charge account.

At the end of her summer's teaching she went in to pay her bill. Mr. Marion Hay, co-owner of the store, who knew she had been asked to teach in Wilbur the following year, said, "You just keep your money for now, Miss Green. We want you to be sure to have enough to come back to Washington. You can pay us after you return." Mr. Hay later became the governor of the State of Washington.

At the close of the six-months' term in her Missouri school, Mama made ready to return to Wilbur, Washington.

"Miss Green", said the Missouri postmaster after he heard she was leaving, "Do you mind telling me how much you will make out West?"

"Fifty dollars a month," she smiled.

The man looked at Mama with admiration. "I'd go to the end of the world for that."

$\mathcal{M}$ainly About Papa

Papa, named William Price Gray, was born April 7, 1878, in Astoria, Oregon. He was the eldest of three brothers, the younger two being David and Clair. Their parents were Samuel Gray and Mary Anne Howe Gray. Papa's grandfather came with his parents from Ohio to Astoria, Oregon, in 1847. His mother, Mary Ann, whose family were originally from North Carolina and Kentucky, came from Missouri to Oregon a few years later.

Mary Anne and her twin brother David were among the eight children born to Joseph and Rebecca Price Howe. In a family genealogy the name Price appears frequently, so that's surely where Papa got his middle name. And since Papa's mother was a twin, a genetic propensity toward twins on Papa's side of the family seems not out of the question.

The Samuel Gray family migrated to Idaho before finally moving to Washington. Papa's father tried his hand at many things, but like his colonial ancestor Howe, whose Wayside Inn was immortalized by Longfellow, Grandpa Samuel Gray ended his days as a hotel keeper. Colonel Ezekiel Howe's sword from the battle of Concord didn't grace the walls of Samuel Gray's hotel as it had the Wayside Inn, nor was the coat of arms with the three wolves' heads anywhere to be seen. In fact, the hotel itself was more like a boarding house. It was in the white and Indian settlement on the Sand Poil River about twenty miles north of Wilbur, in the town of Keller.

But it was while his family was living near Lake Coeur d'Alene in Idaho that Papa had earned his first money as a farm hand. He had almost as much trouble collecting it as he had earning it, but the experience gained then undoubtedly contributed to his later ability as a first-class collector.

A young friend, who already had been hired to do farm work, persuaded Papa to accompany him to the farm and to try for a job. Papa was only about eleven or twelve years of age at that time.

Papa dictated his story to me in the early 1950's.

"Bothwell had worked for these people before, and he assured me that he could get me a job. So my father took a row boat and transported us up to Rockford Point on Coeur d'Alene Lake. From there we walked out to this man Dimmitt's farm. I would say that was about ten miles from the lake—so as soon as we landed, we put our packs on our backs and started out.

"It happened to be on the Coeur d'Alene Indian Reservation, where a good many cattle were being run by the Indians. Where the cattle would sink into the wet swampy ground and pull their hoofs out, there'd be big holes. It seemed to me I must have hit every other hole, and I was wet and tired as could be.

"We finally reached a farmhouse right off the Reservation, where we stayed all night. Next morning we packed our blankets and walked the balance of the distance to the Dimmitts', where I was supposed to get a job. We slept in the barn that night.

"After breakfast next morning, the folks sat around the table and I went outside. My friend stayed with them. He had been promised a job—I had not—so, fifty miles away from home, with no job and no money, I was standing against the house, pretty blue, when the boss came out.

"He said he would give me a try, and, if I could do the work as well as the rest of the help, it would be okay. My friend assured him that I could, but the farmer wasn't sure. He said

10

that I was so small. 'But,' he added, 'if you can do the work, I'll allow you one dollar a day and board.' The following morning he gave me three horses and a plow.

"That first morning Mr. Dimmitt got pretty mad at me. I plowed so much faster with the lead foot plow and could turn three horses around corners so much faster than the other drivers could turn six, that I was catching up with them before noon.

" 'Damn it,' said Dimmitt, 'A kid's a kid, and you can't make a man out of him!'

"I'd nearly killed his horses.

"However, at the end of thirty-six days he told me that I had done a good job, and did allow me a dollar a day that summer, just as he was paying the other men. But—and here's the catch—he said, 'I haven't any money. I was in at the bank this morning and they wouldn't let me have any money to pay off my help.'

"He told us we had to wait until fall when the wheat was threshed, but I said, 'Mr. Dimmitt, I walked out here and I wonder if you could get a pony for me so I could ride back?'

"He assured me that he could, for the amount of seven dollars and a half to be deducted from my wages. I put my blankets on the pony the next morning and rode him home.

"When fall came, we received a letter saying we would receive our wages the next week. Instead of waiting for him to send a check, I took a four-horse team from home and drove out to see Mr. Dimmitt. When the wheat was threshed , I took my wages in wheat. I hauled it to the mill in Rockford and traded it for flour, which I loaded pretty well to the front of the wagon before starting the trip home.

"On the way, while driving down a steep hill, the brakes didn't hold very well, on account of the weight being forward, when suddenly the root of a tree was sticking out of the hill at the side of the road. The horses shied and I was thrown forward off the high seat of the wagon. The front wheel ran over my heel, across the inside, cracking the bone. The back wheel ran across my right side, but the weight was all in the front wheels, so that didn't hurt much. I yelled *'Whoa'* and the old team stopped.

"That was pretty near the end of the story, because from there on I mounted the wagon again and drove on home with my flour."

No wonder Papa met challenges so well. He'd begun his training early! Then Papa recounted the following with satisfaction:

"When I was fourteen years old, our family was living on a quarter section wheat ranch on the Coeur d'Alene Reservation about three miles from Fort Sherman.

"My father took a job for me to break horses for the soldiers who were stationed there. Fifteen head of horses were brought to the ranch and I broke them! I put them through their paces every day until time for the inspection back at the fort.

"Each horse had to pass three tests. For the first test, the rider had to walk the horse away from the judges about a hundred feet, than back. Test two—Trot away and back. Test three—run away and back—this to test the horse's wind. Well, I rode all fifteen through inspection, and everyone passed! I was paid $15 a head, and when the Spanish American War broke out, those horses were ready!

"I stayed on at the Fort, working for my room and keep so that I could go to the Government school there. I lived with the Quarter-Master Sergeant. All I had to do was milk two cows a day and take the mail between the Fort and the Northern Pacific Railroad. I was furnished cart and horse for this, but milking one of the cows wasn't so easy. She was a kicker.

"A fellow by the name of Merritt, who was kind of a

flunky and managed cows for the officers, heard about my kicking cow. Well, he suggested he should come over and show me how to manage that animal.

"The stall was about three feet wide, just room for the cow and the milker. Merritt stuck his head in her flank, said, 'So-o-o-o Bossy', and just as he was starting to milk her, that cow reached up with her hind foot, started kicking until she kicked him right out of the barn.

"It wasn't long until every soldier in the Fort knew that Merritt had been kicked right out the barn door."

For those jobs, which made it possible for Papa to go to school, he was paid ten dollars a month, in addition to his room and board.

It was a rare occasion when Papa recounted his experience breaking wild horses at fifteen dollars a head for the army or rolling logs on Lake Coeur d'Alene. Only occasionally did he refer to the early 1900's when he drove a freight stage with six horses over the winding, steep and narrow road that led into the Indian country north of Wilbur. Nor did he often tell how on snowy, slippery nights, he reined his horses so that the stage tongue was headed toward the inside wall of the canyon. He stood atop his load of goods, his coat off, the cold wind biting into him as the freight stage careened down the slippery three-quarter mile grade. He braced himself in order that he might jump to safety if his horses slipped or if the stage started rolling over the steep banks and into the canyons below.

Baseball

Never once did Papa doubt his ability to handle challenging situations. Baseball handed him an interesting one. With his family recently moved to Keller, there Papa rounded up four sets of brothers. They were the essence of a baseball nine to whip the world they played in. They did that when they beat Almira.

Papa's ability as a player caused the manager of the Wilbur Nine to offer him a job, plus a contract for ten dollars a game if he would move to Wilbur and catch for their team. That was in 1901.

The game that brought about the offer was between Keller and Almira, a town about fourteen miles to the west of Wilbur.

All week Papa had been working at Meteor Camp, an old lead mine in the Keller hills. He was riding back home to spend Sunday at home, unaware that there was to be a ball game, when he stopped for a drink of water at the shack of an old miner.

"Bill, better hurry up and git down to Keller," the old man said, "Jist come from there and they're awantin' you to play ball."

"Who's playing?"

"Keller and Almira, and your team's in purty bad shape."

Tired as he was, Papa jumped onto his horse and galloped to the flat place above Keller where the game was in progress.

The score was thirteen to two, in favor of the visitors.

"Git in there, Bill," the Keller fans yelled.

He didn't have spiked shoes or a suit, but he stripped off his chaps and his leather vest, kicked off his heavy boots, and borrowing some moccasins from one of the Indian onlookers, he went to the catcher's mound to replace the young fellow who had never caught before.

The pitcher was a half-breed whose pitches were fast as streaked lightning, but completely unpredictable in their wildness. It was no wonder that the other catcher hadn't been able to catch them.

"Look out," Papa warned the first batter, "Don't let this fellow hit you. It would kill you if he did."

"Don't you worry about me, son. I'm watching," the batter said as he kept edging away from the plate.

"Look out," Papa warned as he jumped to catch the wild pitch, and the man backed farther away. After three balls and three strikes he was out.

A succession of batters followed; the same business was repeated. By the end of the seventh inning, after catching balls high, low, out and in from the plate in a barrage of consistently inconsistent fast pitches, Papa was exhausted, ready to sit on the bench and recuperate. That was when "E. T.", the manager of the Wilbur team who had been watching the game, said, "For God's sake, stay with it. Nobody else can catch that fellow's balls."

Papa stayed with it. The final score was fifteen to thirteen in favor of Keller! That was when E. T. Hay offered him the job in Wilbur—$10 a game plus a job.

Papa rode twenty-five miles to get there. The next morning he went to work at the local depot, loading freight and handling baggage for forty-five dollars a month. But, during the baseball season which averaged a couple of games a week, Papa was in the top money bracket for the town!

$\mathcal{M}$iss Green
Becomes Mrs. Gray

While he was a grain buyer for the Columbia River Milling Company, owned by the Hays brothers and their brother-in-law M. E. Alexander, Papa met and began paying some attention to the pretty primary teacher from Missouri. He noticed the blue eyes, clear complexion, and thick brown hair that was referred to as Woman's Crowning Glory. It was inevitable that sooner or later she should fall in love—and she did—with Papa. He must have been a real catch. He was handsome, a good worker —which would have been important to her—and a popular baseball player. "Will," she called him. He was "Bill" to some and "Mr. Gray" to those younger than he, as was in keeping with the custom of the day. He was also four years younger than Della Green (though no one in Wilbur ever knew that until they read her obituary more than fifty years later).

Early pictures of Mama show that she had a real sense of style. But baseball players were popular young men about town. It took Papa nearly three years to realize that undoubtedly if he didn't marry Mama, someone else would be very happy to have her as a wife. They used to meet during their lunch hour to walk back to the schoolhouse together. Green and Gray proved to be a happy color combination. It was on one of those noon-hour walks that he proposed and she accepted.

So on Christmas Day 1904, young Will Gray, grain buyer and ball player, and Miss Della Green, pretty primary teacher, drove to Spokane,

DELLA WRAY GREEN GRAY
EARLY PICTURES OF MAMA SHOW THAT SHE
HAD A REAL SENSE OF STYLE.

nearly seventy miles away, to be joined in the holy bonds of matrimony. The Rev. George Giboney performed the wedding ceremony at his Spokane home. Ironically, that was the same day that Papa's mother died in a Spokane hospital.

The following is from *The Wilbur Register*:

"When Mr. And Mrs. Gray returned home that evening, their joy was turned to sadness by the information that the groom's mother had died that afternoon when a sudden and unexpected relapse from an operation ten days earlier had proved fatal.

"The groom has been in the employ of M. E. & E. T. Hay for several years, in charge of their large grain warehouse during the grain season and is a trusted employee. The bride has been engaged in the Wilbur Schools for the past six years. Her continued service is an indication of the esteem in which she is held by the board and all the patrons of the school.

"Their friends are legion all of whom, including the Register, are freely bestowing the very best of good wishes."

Since married women were not by choice hired to teach children in those days, that tribute spoke eloquently of her skill.

About Business

Before Papa and Mama married and took up housekeeping in the four room house a block off Main Street, Papa, during his varied career, had some valuable experiences as a clerk in Wilbur's General Store. After marrying, they both felt that, when they could afford it, they would like to own a business of their own. A business of their own would seem to offer the safest guarantee that they would be able to provide the best educational opportunities available for the family they planned to have. Education—the pot of gold at the end of the rainbow.

Papa counted the experiences he gained clerking as belonging on the credit side of the ledger, better fitting him for the independent business man that he hoped to become.

One such incident occurred in Parrish's General store, where Mr. Parrish overlooked his domain from the bookkeeper's cage on the low balcony at the back of his store. Mr. Parrish kept the books and an eye on the business. Papa clerked down below. People liked to have the handsome young man wait on them because, with the true business man's acumen, he was anxious that the customers find exactly what they wanted.

It was a Saturday morning when a short well-built fellow with a ruddy face came into the store.

"What can I do for you, sir?" Papa greeted him.

"I want to buy the best suit in the house." The gentleman accentuated the word *best* with a nod of his head.

Papa looked him over appreciatively and recalled a very fine gray suit of excellent material and, if he judged correctly, in the customer's size.

"I think we have just what you want," he told the man. "If you'll step back here, I'll show you."

The gray suit was taken from the rack and its excellent qualities pointed out to the prospective buyer. The man tried it on and it fit perfectly.

"I'll take it," the man said without so much as asking the price, and Papa laid it on the counter.

"Is there anything else I can help you with?"

"I want six pairs of wool socks and two suits of your best underwear." The man had Papa lay the merchandise with the suit. "Now I want the best leather grip in the store."

That filled the needs of this apparently free spending customer, so the merchandise was wrapped and Papa totaled the bill. It came to more than fifty dollars.

Papa told him, and the customer didn't bat an eye. "You can just charge that to me, young man."

"Just a minute, sir," Papa hurried to explain, "I'll have to check with Mr. Parrish." He went to the stairs and called up to the owner.

The old gentleman pulled his glasses down on his nose and looked out over his cage on the balcony. "Yes, Will?"

"Uh, this gentleman over here has just picked out fifty-four dollars' worth of merchandise, and he'd like to charge it. Will that be all right?"

Mr. Parrish opened the door of his tiny cubicle and stepped out onto the balcony proper. He adjusted his glasses further on his nose and peered over the railing at the stocky figure below. "Nope, nope," he said, still peering over his glasses. "Don't charge a thing to that man," and the old gentleman went back to his open ledgers.

Papa was very solicitous in rephrasing the blunt refusal. "I'm very sorry but Mr. Parrish says this purchase will have to be cash."

"Well, that's a helluva note," his stocky customer exploded, "after *me* going to all this trouble!"

The Entrepreneurial Plunge

While Mama was still teaching, she one day spoke to the owner of a small newsstand in Wilbur.

"Mr. Burnett, if you ever decide to sell this business, would you let Mr. Gray and me know? We might be interested in buying."

About a year later the man came to Papa. He said that he wanted to get out of business, and Papa and Mama could have that newsstand for the value of the inventory.

Ordinarily that would have sounded like a reasonable offer, but Papa and Mama knew that the newsstand's business had been gradually falling off because of too much competition. Hay's store now carried school supplies, and the town drugstore carried stationery.

For several days they discussed the pitfalls and advantages involved in buying out Mr. Burnett. They wanted a business of their own; they couldn't hope to be in a position to tackle a proposition bigger than the one that was offered them now. Yet, Papa felt that without exclusive rights to certain lines which were now carried by other merchants, the business was too small to show enough profit. That offered a possible solution and a challenge.

Papa went to the biggest businessman first, the man for whom he was buying grain, Mr. M. E. Hay, co-owner of the M. E. & E. T. Hay Department Store.

"Mr. Hay," Papa began, "Mrs. Gray and I were thinking of buying out Mr. Burnett. The present stock is too small to make it pay with the competition which now exists, but if Mrs. Gray and I didn't have to compete with your store in handling school supplies for the town, and you would let us have an exclusive there, I think we could make a go of the business."

Mr. Hay didn't hesitate a minute. His keen eyes sparkled and his decisive mouth with its trim mustache flashed a smile. "Why, of course, Will," he said, "be glad to let you handle the school supplies. I only put in that line because Burnett caters to the wrong crowd." Mr. Hay was a conservative and his stand on liquor differed from what some people termed "the saloon crowd."

"Lots of people don't want to trade with Burnett. I merely put school supplies in as an accommodation to my friends. Be glad to drop out of competition with the newsstand if you folks buy it."

Papa went next to Bandy's Drugstore. Would the owner be willing to give him an exclusive on fine stationery? Mr. Bandy obliged gladly.

The owner of The Golden Rule assured Papa that he would be happy to handle only cheaper candies and let Papa and Mama have the agency for high priced chocolates and boxed candies.

With these obstacles overcome, Papa conferred with the distinguished looking bank president and founder, E. L. Farnsworth, and with the bank treasurer.

"As you gentlemen probably know, Della and I have only three hundred and sixty dollars in our joint savings," he began as he sat facing the two bankers. "But we have a chance to buy the newsstand. The stock inventories at close to fifteen hundred dollars. I've made Mr. Burnett an offer of seventy-five cents on the dollar for it, which he has agreed to take. For the purchase price and money to increase the stock, Della and I are hoping that the bank will lend us fifteen hundred dollars."

"We're mighty glad that you're going in business for yourselves, Will," Mr. Farnsworth, the president told him in his kindly way, "and the bank will be glad to lend you the money."

"I suppose you will want some kind of security?" Papa questioned. The two men looked at one another and smiled, then Mr. Thompson, the treasurer said, "It won't be necessary, Will. Just you and your wife sign the note."

The deal was closed. The Newstand, as they named it, belonged to Papa and Mama. For the next year Papa got up at dawn to deliver the Spokane daily papers on his bicycle before sweeping out the store, returning home for breakfast, and then reporting to work at the warehouse. Mama, as they had planned, took care of the business.

Within a year the note was paid off, but from that purchase of their first business until twenty-two years later, never a year passed by that

Papa didn't borrow money from the bank. He borrowed in order to expand, or to get cash discounts on his purchases, or, on the advice of the bankers, to make investments.

Toward the back of the store was a rocking chair, probably for Mama's comfort. An early picture shows her at one side of the store, her thick brown hair piled high on her head, her hands folded gracefully at her waist as she stands erect in her dark full-sleeved blouse and dark skirt. Papa stands casually against a glass showcase opposite her. Between them is a long white table displaying a variety of popular sheet music of the day.

Their most popular merchandise included sheet music, stationery, post cards, magazines, tobaccos and confectionery. They also had books on open shelves.

$\mathcal{D}$ouble Entry

After eighteen months, the note having been paid off at the bank and a cash business built up, Papa had given up his job as grain buyer to devote all his time to the store. Up until a few weeks before our birth, Mama continued to help him in the store.

She had a pongee coat with a large black collar which, toward the end of that "indelicate period," she never took off, even though we were born in the very middle of summer where the thermometer very often hovered near the ninety-degree mark.

She and Papa had worked out a system, though, whereby he waited on customers in the center and on one side of the store. On the other side, Mama stood behind the tall counters which they had installed to replace the open shelves and tables. That was most successful except on the Sunday afternoon when Papa played ball. Then Mama had to cover the whole store by herself, and the embarrassment she suffered was acute.

Happily, however, on July 30, 1909, her one childbearing experience resulted in William's and my Double Entry into this welcoming world.

We were born just twenty-five minutes apart in the bedroom of a little wooden house off Main Street. I was the earlier, being born at five minutes after noon on that hot summer day. William followed at twelve thirty. Peculiarly, considering our later development, he was an ounce heavier than his twin, tipping the scales at six pounds and one ounce.

Mama could trace at least seven pairs of twins on her side of the family, while Papa knew of one set dangling from a branch of his family tree. They were David and Mary, children of John Howe of North Carolina and his wife Jane Dunlop Howe.

On this auspicious day, when Papa rushed from the house to purchase an extra set of necessities for his twins, he insists he was called a liar more often than he's ever been, before or since.

"Which is it, Will, boy or girl?"

"Both," Papa would respond and hurry on, to the incredulous comments of the villagers. Until he had provided Mama with extra necessities for their babies, Papa didn't even take the time to pass out cigars. He did that later. According to Mama, he was kidded unmercifully and had to hand out two cigars instead of the customary one.

"How are you, Della?" he asked over and over as he looked down at Mama, after the doctor had left things in the charge of a practical nurse.

"Tired, but just fine, Sweetheart." She smiled up at him and then down at the twins. "Did you ever think that we'd be lucky enough to get both our boy and our girl at the same time?"

"Together we can do anything, Della," Papa said, then, "Lord, I've got to get back to the store!"

The engraved announcement of our arrival had the names Helen Marguerite and William Price, Jr. engraved on tiny separate cards, tied with pink or blue ribbons to the left hand corner of the announcement proper.

"Twins" seemed to be a magic word. Gifts in duplicate started coming in. There were three sets of silver napkin rings with our names and year of our birth engraved on them. One set came from the Governor's mansion in Olympia. Mr. M. E. Hay had been elected Lieutenant Governor of the state, and now presided as Governor after the death of the chief executive. There were blankets, and capes, baby books and such, all of which delighted the brand new parents.

After our arrival Mama had a full time job at home. Lots of innocents who had never experienced bringing up twins said, "Well, two are just as easy as one."

Mama didn't agree with that theory. Feedings (for awhile Mama breast-fed us, until I began to cry all the time and got dark circles under my eyes) took endless time. There was twice as much washing, and she'd just get one of her babies bundled up to go for a ride in the twin buggy when they other one would have to be taken out and changed.

In those days too, mothers of babies didn't grab a coat and go for a walk in bobby-socks and a sweater and skirt. Pictures of Mama and a friend of hers who had only one baby in her perambulator, showed the ladies with enormous hats atop their high piled hair, fitted jackets or long coats over starched white shirt-waists with high collars, and long sweeping skirts cinching in comparatively small waists. Under those clothes were worn corsets, long stockings, chemises and petticoats. Ladies' laced shoes were high topped! When just dressing took so much time, it isn't surprising that Mama looked older in some of our early pictures than she did years later.

🙢

By the time we were a year and a half old, Papa had gone to his bankers again. He did this each fall when he borrowed to buy school books and supplies, and each November when he needed money to pay for Christmas stock. This time he borrowed to expand and move his business. The town weekly, *The Register*, stated in 1911:

> "Will Gray made a commendable move when he moved
> his Newstand......"

In the meantime, he had received his 18" x 24" inch diploma from Lewis Commercial School certifying that he had completed their prescribed course "in Practical Double Entry Bookkeeping...giving satisfactory evidence that he could Open, Conduct and Close a Set of Books according to that method." That knowledge served him well through the succeeding years.

The store had additional floor space and new lines of goods— Kodaks which accounted for the hundreds of pictures that Papa took when we were growing up, sheet music, Columbia Grafanolas and records. Because he was still a baseball enthusiast and a member of the Wilbur team, Papa carried a complete line of Spalding baseball equipment. After the twins arrival, Papa had put in Christmas toys.

25

Chistmas Recollections

Christmas eve at our church with Wise Men and Mary and Joseph kneeling by the manger, stockings filled with oranges, nuts and hard candy, and Christmas carols sung by us all—these, and our own gifts for mission boxes which we piled under the tree in front of the choir box, were all a part of our childhood.

After the service, Mama, William and I would walk over to the store to hurry Papa home, so we could have our tree that evening. That was so Papa could sleep late on Christmas morning.

Santa still left us a stocking full of necessary remembrances for Christmas morn. That gave Papa lots of extra sleep, not having to get up early to enjoy the sight of his twins opening their one or two special presents—often items that had stayed in the store's showcase until Christmas eve.

One Christmas morning, when we were five or six years old, a pink, shiny box of chocolate peppermints protruded from my stocking. "To Helen from Santa," it read. I recognized Mama's handwriting and felt rather pleased with myself. Each year I felt sure that the toys Santa brought were the same as those I'd seen in the store before Christmas. Somehow I knew Papa and Mama had been working together with Santa for a very long time.

The House

Mama couldn't help Papa at the store any more, but she did enter a newspaper subscription-selling contest when William and I were two years old. The prize was an Overland sedan! With Papa's help and the use of the telephone, Mama won the car. They needed a larger house much more than an Overland sedan, so Papa offered the owner of a then handsome seven-room house the car and four hundred dollars cash in trade. The man accepted, and Papa was in debt some more, for he had to borrow the cash from the bank.

The house had gingerbread around the edge of the flat, front-porch roof, and gingerbread under the gables. The plate glass parlor window was bordered at the top with little squares of varicolored glass.

The front door had a delicately frosted window in the upper half, and opened into our central hall with oak stairs and the railing that served William and me as a slide, sometimes. Behind the living room was a room which Mama used as the downstairs bedroom when we were babies. Later it was the den with a couch in it, where we sometimes took our afternoon naps. Much later the partition between it and the front room was removed and Mama had a room large enough for all the furniture that she just couldn't seem to discard, plus the new pieces acquired over the years. Upstairs were the three regular bedrooms off a pleasant hall.

When we were little, there was a small wooden structure at the southeast corner of the yard. It had a seat with two holes over a pit, which smelled of lye. It had half moon cutouts, high up on two walls, and a supply of slippery mail order catalogue pages, which were not for reading only. That was before Papa installed a full bathroom and later a toilet in the laundry room off the kitchen.

On the other side of the kitchen there was a pantry with dish cupboards whose glass doors were accessible from the dining room.

Outside the kitchen door and just a step from the back porch was the stone cellar. When we lifted the iron latch and pushed open the thick wooden door, the smell of damp earth was mingled with the pungency of sauerkraut, vegetables, and apples. Mama's canned goods filled the shelves. She kept her cleaning solvent in there too, and ice, when we had it, was stored in a galvanized tub with burlap over it.

A fine old cherry tree touched the dirt roof of our cellar with its reaching limbs. Old fashioned flowers grew on top. In the early summer, bees and humming birds whirred among the blossoms of the yellow currant or drew nectar from the fragrant blossoms of the pear or apple trees.

As William and I opened our eyes many mornings, it was apt to be to the sound of Mama singing,

"Good morning, merry sunshine,
How did you wake so soon?

You scared away the little stars
And chased away the moon."

As she continued the song we'd stretch our little bodies contentedly, conscious of the fresh clean morning air, and the sun drifting through the curtained windows. Outside we would see the apple trees and smell the dewy grass. The robins chirped in the trees and an occasional meadowlark sounded its melodious whistle not far away.

That was the house where we grew up, the one in which Papa and Mama gave us our first allowances, part to be put in the bank "for your college education." This was the "pot of gold at the end of the rainbow." It would enable us to prepare for life's problems and opportunities most effectively.

Life With Mama and Papa

On certain occasions Mama's patience, her quotations and her reasoning didn't influence us as she hoped. Papa would then combine a firm hand on our derrieres with an unimpassioned talk afterwards on why he had to dispense such punishment.

There was the occasion of our running away when we were two or three years old. Mama was hanging up clothes in the side yard when she missed us one day. She called; she searched around our house and up and down the street and on the hill above, with no success. Finally after becoming increasingly frantic, she sent word to Papa at the store. He locked up and came pedaling home on his bicycle.

While covering the south side of town Papa finally found us on the hill, three blocks west of home. We were having a wonderful time with a little girl, older than we were, who was visiting her grandfather.

Papa not only made us physically uncomfortable but he shamed us in front of the little red head who had been willing to play with us even though we weren't as old as she was. But by the time he had escorted us home, taken us on his knee and told us that it had hurt him more than it did us—that was hard to believe—we understood that home was the best place to be.

The Twins

From the time we were three years old, I began to develop into the husky athletic one of the twins. I grew taller and heavier, while William was less robust. If he fell down, I pulled him up to carry him, protesting, to Mama or Papa.

A policeman in Spokane admonished Mama for making her little girl carry "that heavy suitcase." Mama had tried to prevent me from doing it, but it was far easier to let me continue than to go down the street holding William by one hand and trying to wrestle the case from me with the other hand.

I caught all the contagious diseases first, always in a mild form. Then after the proper period of incubation William came down with the worst case in town. Aside from that he suffered from chronic appendicitis, and Mama was afraid to have such a little fellow operated on.

Papa took lots of pictures of us. One of them—now this book's cover—was a 12" x 16" sepia enlargement by Kodak. Framed in a wide concave oak frame, it hung above the Kodak display case at the store. It hangs above my desk now, and I smile when I look at it. Papa must have just grabbed his Kodak, shepherded his twins across the street to the stretch of grass beside the stone and brick bank building which served as a backdrop, and snapped us. And so we stood, dressed alike but for knee-length bloomers showing below William's belted dress.

Already an inch or more shorter than I, he had his right arm behind my left shoulder and his hand around my neck. His head was tipped lovingly toward my shoulder as he obligingly smiled at Papa. His loose white belt was sagging down left, and his crocheted cap with side tassel rimmed his Dutch-bob bangs, as we were recorded for posterity. Black stockings and sandals encased our underpinnings.

My dress, like his, was pleated at the bottom; the wide collars and short sleeves were rimmed with braid. I think the picture was taken on one of the first hot days, for my forearms were pale down to just above the wrist, but my hands and wrists were a translucent brown and I don't think it was dirt.

But what I love about the picture is that it tells so much about how people might have perceived us. There stood William, happy, self-possessed, so likable. Then me. I look happy too, and self possessed, but with my feet planted firmly apart, my crocheted cap on the back of my head and a big smile. I look like a husky well-fed kid ready for anything. William makes you want to do something nice for him. As for me, my grin seems to say, "What's next? I'm ready."

When we twins dressed alike people knew we were twins, and we were asked to do such things as drive a team of goats around the track at the Wilbur Fair—at least sit in the little goat cart and hold the reins while the owner, who also had a trained bear, walked beside us. But after Mama finally agreed with Papa that William should go to the barber for a regular boy's haircut, and our dress-alike suits were discontinued, we weren't asked to do things as twins anymore. William and I had lost the only features that ever made the Gray Twins nearly identical—clothes and haircuts.

After the trip to the barber, nobody but the Indian squaws from the Nespelum Reservation could tell we were twins. When they came to our door, William and I stood big-eyed listening to them barter for money or clothes in exchange for a ten-pound lard pail full of shiny purple huckleberries. After they and Mama had completed their negotiations the squaws would look at us and cluck and chuckle and nod their heads.

"Twins?" they'd say in a way that made their question a statement.

"Yes," Mama admitted. "How did you know?"

They would cluck and chuckle some more, nod their heads and

30

say, "Twins."

Mama had to be satisfied with that, but whenever other people said, "My, you'd certainly never think the children are twins." Mama's stock reply was, "Well, the Indians can always seem to tell they are." That was true, though nobody ever knew how they did it.

Until William grew taller than I—which wasn't until late college years—it was not uncommon for someone to say, "Billy, you certainly don't look as old as your sister." (Only the family consistently called him William until we were grown up.)

Instead of resenting the reminder that he was smaller than his twin, he merely grinned and explained, "That's because I hold my age so well." I, while impatiently awaiting our sixteenth birthday, simply interpreted such observations as a tribute to my sophistication.

HELEN AND WILLIAM, AGE 2 YEARS AND 10 MONTHS
ON MAIN STREET IN FRONT OF THE STATE BANK OF WILBUR.
1912 POSTCARD PHOTO BY W. P. GRAY

$\mathcal{M}ain$ Street and Beyond

By 1910, Wilbur's population was around seven hundred. The weekly *Register* carried notices of traveling theatricals playing *East Lynn* for four nights in the G. A. R. Hall, of dog and monkey shows which performed in a tent, or musical trios of world fame. Evangelists came to town and yearly fairs were held.

Stories of the murder of a half-breed Indian by a Finn over the affections of a white girl in the country north of town made the front page. There was the story of seventeen year old, ninety pound Lizzie who stole two horses and a buggy from a livery stable in an effort to get back to the coast, and news of the doctor from a neighboring town who was tarred and feathered for rape.

Middle westerners came out West to invest in wheat lands. M. E. Hay had made a fortune by buying the farmers' wheat and selling them farm equipment, clothes and staples. Afterwards as governor of the state of Washington his speeches and views appeared in print each Thursday in the local paper.

Hay's Department Store

Founded in the early 1890's, Hay's Department Store developed into one of the largest stores in eastern Washington. It was unique, handling "everything from a needle to a threshing machine."

Inside the store, people could go directly from one department to the next—from furniture to hardware to the grocery store. From groceries one went directly into dry goods and the clothing department with the millinery shop and bookkeeper's cage on the mezzanine. Those departments, with the many aisles and tables for bolts of cloth and linens, took up the largest area of the complex. Shoes for the family, coats and dresses, overalls and work shirts, patterns, hats, needles and pins, bedding and underwear were staples.

The undertaking parlor, which was owned by Mr. Lyse, was behind his furniture department at the east end of the building.

The hardware department's tall moveable ladder, that slid along a track from the front end of the store to the back, leaned against the west wall. That was lined with dozens of labeled drawers, holding screws and nails and all the small hardware necessary for the repair and maintenance of farm machinery. Coleman lanterns, coils of chain, and barrels of spikes were part of the stock that farmers could count on finding in the store. Behind the store the whole area was fenced to encompass large pieces of John Deere farm machinery displayed there.

In the back of the dry goods section hung ready-made dresses and coats. Full-length mirrors in golden oak frames reflected the people who passed in front of them. Hats were back there too, and the shoe department where I bought my first high heels.

Upstairs was the office where our Sunday School treasurer, Mr. Owen, kept the books.

The store was purposely built several feet off the ground with the sidewalks proportionately high in order that farmers might easily load their wagons from the walk. At either end of the block short wooden inclines led down to the street. Through the spaces between boards of the walk, silt, the dust, and the rain easily filtered through. Under there boys hunted for money that had been dropped. Hay's Department Store was truly the closest thing to a mall that Wilbur ever had.

A 1912 picture of Wilbur's Main Street shows a remarkable variety of businesses. In the west block were Bandy's Drug Store, Sherman Clay's, Wilbur Meat Company, the Wilbur Bank, and the Livery and Feed Stable. Lawyer Love, who had two large Airedale dogs, had his office above Bandy's Drug Store.

WILBUR FAIR, OCTOBER 1912

Unpictured was the Madsen Hotel, with both sleeping rooms and a dining room to serve townspeople and travelers.

In the east block were Gray's Newstand (which had outgrown its original location) and the M. E. & E. T. Hay Department Store, which took up three-quarters of the block. On the other side of the street was Bump's pool hall. The brick grocery store with the lodge hall above was at the far end of the block. Around the corner was the post office.

South of Main Street was the Chinese laundry, where Mama took Papa's stiff collars and shirts to be laundered. Beyond that lay the railroad tracks on which the Northern Pacific Railroad brought mail, passengers and freight. The ice house, past the red depot, was where the engines stopped.

Freight trains arrived early in the day to load wheat from the grain warehouses bordering the tracks, or to load flour from the Columbia River Milling Company.

The afternoon train's familiar whistle alerted inhabitants that passengers, mail and freight were soon to be deposited or loaded from the station's broad planked platform. Inside the depot, the station master, with gartered sleeves and green eye-shade, tended to the intermittent click-clack-click of the telegraph, answered the phone or sold tickets through the tiny office window.

For some townspeople, watching the arrival of the train was a daily ritual. Each afternoon at the sound of the *"Wh-ooo Who—ooooo"* of the approaching train, the curious gathered on the station platform. There they could be sure of being the first to know what happened when the trains pulled into town.

Fire!

Mama, William and I had been visiting our cousin Doris, Aunt Jessie and Uncle Wallace Anderson in Spokane. While we were away, Papa ate his meals at the hotel. He was there shortly after noon when, at the wail of the fire siren, the dining room emptied in minutes. Outside could be seen gray smoke pouring from a roof top near the center of town.

"It looks like my place!" Papa called to the people around him and he jumped on his bicycle to race to the scene.

It was the Newstand. The building was filled with smoke. A few flames licked the sky. Boys and men were carrying merchandise out of the building. Suddenly Papa saw two strangers lugging something heavy between them. It was the cash register. Before he could stop them, Mr. E. L. Farnsworth, the banker, stepped in front of the men.

"Let that alone!" he ordered. Then he and another man carried it across the street, up the stone steps and inside the bank for safety.

The first thing seen by Mama, William and me, returning by train from our visit, was the heavy gray smoke billowing upward. The station master told Mama it was from the Newstand.

We hurried toward Main Street where firemen were trying to control the fire. People milled about looking at the hundreds of dollars worth of merchandise which lined the street.

When the insurance adjuster came, Papa said, "There's just one item that I know of that's missing, and I don't know whether your company takes care of losses like this or not. A Kodak was evidently

36

stolen during the fire."

Papa always numbered each Kodak and registered the number in a little black notebook. When the Kodak was sold, the number was checked off. After the fire an $18 Kodak was missing. The insurance adjuster said that his company would cover its loss.

About twelve years later a gentleman came into our place of business. "Hello, Mr. Gray," he said. " I don't think you remember me, but my boy and I lived here at the time of your fire, years ago.

"Do you remember that Kodak you gave him for helping you the day of the fire? Well, sir, he still has that Kodak, and he thinks it's the finest Kodak in the world."

"Well," Papa said, "I'm glad he's been able to enjoy it. Yes, Sir," he mused, "that was quite a fire."

For a few months after that fire, limited business was carried on in the rented space in the now nearly-empty Hay building. After cars made travel easy, people drove to Spokane, only seventy miles away, for shopping. Other stores duplicated grocery and dry goods departments; mail order houses took their share. Finally only the hardware department remained in Hays Department Store. Papa was fortunate to have that extra store space in which to carry on limited business. When the new building was ready on the site of the old one, Gray's Newstand reopened for business.

The Baseball Legend

From the late 1800's through the 1930's when every small town had its baseball team, games between small towns had elements of danger. Pitched balls aimed at the best batters took Papa and other strong players out of the game with a broken bone, more than once, as reported in the weekly *Register*. But those were not the games for which Papa was remembered. His unforgettable game took place in 1911, the result of controversy between the Wilbur and Sprague teams. It was mutually agreed on a rematch on neutral territory. The site was Natatorium Park's ballpark in Spokane. The stakes were $1,000 —winner take all.

Papa was the team's best first-baseman, also the best catcher. For the big game, a catcher from Waterville was asked to fill in behind the plate.

The catcher said he couldn't; he had to work. After talking to his employer, he said he could; his boss would let him off.

A few days later he said he couldn't; his wife wanted him home for a dinner party. The wife was called; she said he could. The catcher agreed to come.

The day of the game, the Waterville catcher didn't arrive in Wilbur to go with the team as expected. In Spokane he never showed up.

With Ettinborough playing first base, Papa took over the catcher's position.

It was the last of the ninth inning; the score 2 to 2, Wilbur up to bat. The pitcher McCluskey, first man up, bunted safely. Ettinborough did the same. With men on first and second, the manager had the third man

WILBUR TEAM WON $1,000 IN 1911 BALL GAME AGAINST SPRAGUE AT
NATATORIUM PARK, SPOKANE. CATCHER: W. P. GRAY (CENTER ROW, RIGHT)

bunt. It proved to be a sacrifice.

Papa was up next. With one swing of his bat, he hit a clean line drive over the short stop. McCluskey was in, and, to the roar of the crowd, Wilbur won the game!

The team collected $1,000 and immediately hired a photographer to immortalize the winners of the great event. In the picture Papa, at the right end of the center row, is smiling the sweetest smile; his catcher's mask, mitt and bat lie prominently on the floor in front of the team.

I cherish the picture. That was the day Papa's hit made him a baseball legend in Wilbur and the surrounding country.

Mama at Bat

It was from those days that baseball fans remembered Papa. With Mama it was different. She played at least one time and was remembered for it. It was one of the few times she ever faced a challenge unprepared.

That was because when Papa played ball, Mama was usually at the store. What she knew best about baseball was that when Papa kept pulling a ligament in one leg toward the end of his playing days, the store smelled like liniment. (He'd massage it with the smelly stuff in his office after a game.)

Nearly every summer Mama's and Papa's lodges had a picnic in Pioneer Park, about a mile from town. There under the tall poplars were the sawhorse tables laden with home-cooked food. After dinner of browned chicken, baked beans, homemade pickles, deviled eggs, potato salads, jellos, pies, cakes and ice cream, we kids scampered off to climb the park trees or race up and down the wooden seats of the grandstand. Some of the men pitched horseshoes while others congregated at the ball grounds.

When the ladies walked over, the entertainment committee announced a ladies' ball game. Mama didn't want to play. She liked to feel in command of any situation in which she participated. Though she'd watched Papa in many games before they were married, she was not a player. Despite her protests she was assigned to a team and put up to bat first.

"Come on now, Mrs. Gray," Papa called. "Its all in fun."

Mama wasn't so sure. She protested. She didn't even know how to hold the bat.

Papa came to her rescue. He picked up a light bat and stood beside her. "Let's see how you hold this one, Della. That's fine. Now get about here."

Mama stepped gingerly into position. "Now then, hold your bat over your shoulder, keep your eye on the pitcher, and when she throws the ball—if it's right where you want it—hit it!"

"Pl-a-ay ball!" yelled the umpire. Papa retired to the sidelines. Mama nervously waited for the first throw.

"You ready, Mrs. Gray?" Belle, the pitcher called.

"I guess so," Mama called back, fully aware that she was on her own now.

Belle pitched one over the plate. Mama swung and hit it! And then just stood there.

"*Run, Mrs. Gray,*" called the crowd. "*Run!*" Mama looked befuddled.

"*R-u-n-n!*" They yelled. Mama looked for Papa. He was yelling, too.

"*R-u-u-u-n!!!*" The whole crowd pleaded.

She didn't move.

"*Don't I get three strikes?*" she asked.

Sometimes Papa teased Mama about that ball game. "My Lord, Della," he'd shake his head in disbelief.

"Now, Will. You said yourself it was all in fun."

She'd tell their listeners, "Why before we were married I used to go to ball games with Will all the time. I don't know how I ever did such a thing,"

"You should have seen her the next time," Papa teased, "she made another hit and started sprinting left, toward third base!"

"Oh, pshaw, Will, you know very well I did no such thing."

"No, you did pretty well, Della," Papa would finally admit, a little bit proudly.

That made it all right. Mama had once again proved herself on top of a challenging situation.

$\mathcal{M}$emories, Good or Bad

Books

Papa and Mama believed in the value of good books and music in the home. Consequently our library was an important part of our home life. Mama was the one who read to William and me—from the time we could appreciate the sing-song rhythm of nursery rhymes until we preferred to read to ourselves. While Papa encouraged her to bring home the books she wanted, he allowed William and me to pick out many of the records for our Grafonola. Our records ranged from operatic selections to "Yoocha Hula, Hicky Dula" and "Beautiful Ohio". Those were the kind I danced to.

Much of the knowledge from our books was imparted to us through the quotations or stories which Mama always seemed to have for most any occasion. These ranged from quotes like "To err is human, to forgive divine" and "Handsome is as handsome does" to "He who calleth his brother a fool is in danger of hell fire." The last was for me.

Along side volumes of *The World's Greatest Literature*, our four-tiered oak bookcase with its glass doors held *The Junior Classics* and illustrated stories of *Little Black Sambo* and *Bunnie Cotton Tail*. The book of *Emmy Lou*, which Mama had used when she was teaching, was there beside my volume of Ibsen's *A Doll's House*, bound in red leather. It had been given to me by a fond uncle while I was still in the doll-playing stage!

WILLIAM, MAMA, HELEN, AT HOME BY THE BOOKCASE.
POSTCARD PHOTO BY W. P. GRAY, ABOUT 1913

Snow Times

I remember the Flexible Flyer sled that William and I shared when
we were in the early grades. It was high off the ground and stubby compared to the later ones. It looked big and easily held the two of us, one
lying down to guide it, the other shoving off then kneeling behind as we
started at the top of the Foley hill.

We shared the sled, taking turns if we didn't want to go double. That
is until Papa came home one night for dinner to hear that I wouldn't let
William have his number of turns. Papa rewarded my unwillingness to
cooperate by outright giving the Flexible Flyer to me!

The next day he brought home the biggest, the finest Flyer money
could buy. Papa gave that one to William.

I tearfully threatened to take an ax and chop my brother's sled down to
the size of mine. I was restrained, however—no doubt by Mama and Papa's
seldom-resorted-to but always-carried-out threat of a spanking.

I learned then that *might* does not necessarily mean *right*; for
although I was stronger and larger than William, he came out the winner on that one.

43

The Foley Hill, which accommodated most of the residential traffic from the south hill, was the Mecca for sledders of all ages when the snows came. Big kids would give their sleds a huge pu-s-h-h at the school house or, a block below, they'd jump on and steer their Flexible Fliers and homemade toboggans as they zoomed down the hill, around its two bends, down again for three or four blocks and over the railroad tracks.

Lots of us started our sleds below the bend in the road, a block and a half below the school. We couldn't coast as far as the older boys did, but we loved it. We watched for autos and yelled "Ca-a-r-r-r-s!" whenever we saw one coming. Occasionally a farmer's heavy sleigh on runners would approach, bells on the horses' harness jingling to their rhythmic gait. We'd run to hitch onto the back end and get a free ride to or from the Graingrowers' Warehouse, which sold hay and feed to its customers.

Time meant nothing to sledders on weekends and non-school days. Whether in grade school or high school, we'd stay out until our mittens and socks were soaked and cold; then we'd trudge home for a change.

One of the cars Papa said we should always watch for on the Foley Hill—whether on sleds, wheels or on foot—was driven by the meekest appearing banker in the business. In the teller's cage Mr. Godfrey Thompson's head was generally tipped to one side in a conciliatory manner, as if he wanted us to know that he had our interests at heart.

But he drove with an abandon that warned those in the car's path to get out of the way—fast!

Like some of the big boys who drove over the speed limit, he added to the excitement that gave life in a small town a flavor of its own.

Papa's Fedoras and Politics

Besides his devotion to his family, the business and baseball, Papa loved politics. He was a dyed-in-the-wool Republican who won several handsome fedoras betting on presidential candidates.

The last hat I remember his winning was an elegant, cream colored fedora, which he wore with great style. He always carried his six feet of height with grace and assurance, reflecting his satisfaction with life. That

44

was before Woodrow Wilson was voted into office.

What a shock when, one election day, our teacher appeared wearing a Wilson-McAdoo button. I thought all of our friends were Republicans—not that anyone had ever said that. I just knew that the father of one of my classmates, a feisty ball player with whom Papa sometimes disagreed, was a Democrat—but his wife, who was nice, was Republican. Now I knew Miss Pattella, whom I liked very much, was also a Democrat. For a seven year old it was hard to understand.

Looking back on it, I now realize that it provided an early example about why generalizations don't work. They're apt to be wrong!

Walks

On spring afternoons Mama, William and I took walks. Sometimes we followed the railroad tracks. More often our steps led to the cemetery. We'd run fifty steps and walk fifty, counting aloud as we ran. Then we'd turn to walk the fifty steps back toward Mama.

Meadowlarks piped their melodious theme, and occasionally a green and yellow garter snake would slither from its sunny roadside couch into the grass. Above, the sky was softly blue with just puffs of clouds to decorate the ceiling of the town.

The cemetery was about a mile north of Wilbur, and townspeople cherished its solemn beauty. Wide paths sectioned the hallowed area. Fragrant lilacs, wild roses and solicitous trees softened the lines made by the granite and marble headstones of the graves. Our grandparents were buried there, Samuel and Mary Gray. We sometimes took flowers from our yard to lay upon the graves.

Mama often said how much nicer it is to receive flowers while one is alive than after one is gone.

Grandma Yount

Mrs. Yount, a doctor's widow, lived on the west side of Foley Hill. Her back yard adjoined ours. She liked to invite William and me to "keep her company" some afternoons. And we liked to go there, through her back yard with its huge lilac hedge and lots of garden, to the back door where she'd greet us and take us into the front part of her house. She showed us hand painted dishes and a delicate French Haviland tea set that had belonged to her as a child. I loved that set and one day, when I was seven or eight, she gave it to me!

But what William and I both liked was playing three-handed pinochle with her. She was a wild bidder because, as she said, she "liked to see what the widow was like," and we'd both laugh, unless she did that too often, for we liked to get the "widow" once in a while, too.

World War I

When the United States entered World War I in 1917, the list of draftees was posted every morning on the outside of the Newstand. Men would come to look at the list. Everyday I hoped that Papa's name would never be on that list. It never was.

I remember when the false news of an armistice came following World War I. The papers hadn't been signed yet, although Germany had surrendered. William and I pulled our red wagon and waved little American flags as we marched down Main Street with other proud patriots. Surprised, we watched a woman force poor Nick Bill to mount the high cement base of the flagpole that centered Main Street. As the bewildered and guiltless old German stood beneath the stars and stripes, Mrs. Britton gloried in wrapping a long string of sausages round and round his neck.

Powerful still, and filled with shame, is that first memory of too many wars in my lifetime.

William and Smallpox

During the flu epidemic of 1917, a nurse from Spokane cared for Mama, William and me at home, while Papa stayed at the Madsen Hotel. He wore a gauze mask when he brought mail or medicine or food to our house.

Severe nosebleeds kept me abed for days with lots of attention from the nurse. I slept on a cot in Mama's room. William was in his room next door, while the nurse had my room across the hall. That was the only time that I was as sick—or more so than William.

If I contracted anything suspiciously like measles or mumps or

46

chicken pox, it was always in such a light form that Mama probably was never sure whether it was a disease or just perversity cropping out. That is until William came down with the same thing, only hard.

It was during a summer series of Chautauqua entertainment, when we were nine or ten, that we heard such things as Sousa's Band, lectures, and real live actors in a play. Suddenly I developed a spot on my left arm and the same kind on my chest. There was no local epidemic and I felt perfectly healthy, but Mama asked the doctor's widow, whose yard adjoined ours, if she knew what the spots were.

"Looks to me like a food rash," Grandma Yount said. In a few days the spots were gone. After the proper period of incubation, William broke out with hundreds of the same. He, Mama, and I were quarantined in. Papa was quarantined out. William had smallpox.

Miraculously no other cases developed in town. It could have been that there weren't any more pox to go around, William had so many. Blisters covered his body. Instead of eyelids he had beehives. His feet showed no sign of arches, so distended were the bottoms. He hurt, he itched and, when his fever was at its height, he was delirious.

When I went to his room one morning with breakfast, he suddenly raised up from the pillow to stare at me with glassy eyes and he began to babble incoherently. My heart jumped and I was downstairs beside Mama in a flash. After that, Mama took his breakfast up while I washed the dishes, until that phase of the sickness had passed.

As he gradually grew well enough to get out of bed and no longer had to be carried from room to room, William's appetite for teasing returned. We sat in the porch swing one day, when William began needling me. Feeling, no doubt, that his sister wouldn't dare strike anyone in his still delicate condition, my little twin added insult to injury by taking this rare opportunity to give me a poke.

Having been tormented verbally and then insulted physically, I had no respect for the convalescent. With a retaliating punch I blindly hit back. My fist struck one of his still swollen eyes.

What Mama saw, when she appeared in response to his screams of pain, was gruesome. I was frightened at what I had done. I loved him.

47

Now I wondered if my twin would be all right.

Relegated to my room, I think I asked God to make him well, instead of asking Him to "Bless everybody except William and the Kaiser," a not uncommon request previously.

Miraculously he did recover without an obvious pock mark.

Silvering the Stove

An outsider might have thought Papa lazy because he hired a boy to open the store and didn't get up early. Like Mama, both William and I understood that it was because Papa was tired and needed rest from his long hours in our Newstand.

While Mama ran our home, and helped in the store after William and I started school, she knew that she could always stay home when she wanted to.

With Papa it was different. He had to be there seven days a week with little respite. Even in better times when he hired more help, it was a rare day that ended before he had spent twelve or fifteen hours on the business.

On the mornings when he was fully rested, he was lovable and affectionate with his family and "rarin' to go," as he put it. If he didn't get his rest, however, he was preoccupied at the breakfast table.

That was one reason Mama always got up early and built all the fires, while Papa slept late. Then too, aside from the consideration of Papa's disposition, as she often said, "I'd rather build the fires myself than to clean up the mess that Papa makes."

By the time the house was warm, Mama would start calling him.

"Will," she'd call, "it's time to get up. Almost 8:00 o'clock."

Mama never expected any results from the first call, so at 8:15 she'd send one of us children upstairs. "Mama says to get up. It's 8:15."

Papa would grunt and turn over or maybe go to the bathroom and then back to bed.

Usually the smell of coffee and bacon, or bran muffins baking, plus our reminder, "Mama says she's going to put your egg on now," would get Papa downstairs by 8:45 or 9:00, but it was not an easy matter.

The only occasion that I can recall when he rose voluntarily was shortly after Mama silvered the dining room stove, when we were ten or eleven. That time we didn't even call him.

Mama had just had the dining room, next to the entry hall, papered in a soft blue grass-paper. The softwood floors had been painted the color of oak and painstakingly grained to resemble hardwood. With freshly laundered curtains up, the oak dining set in place, and the potted fern in the front window, the room gave just the effect that Mama wanted, until she looked at the coal stove in the corner near the kitchen. That spoiled the picture.

After pondering her problem for several days the thought occurred to her to give the offender a coat of aluminum paint. The finished product was nothing less than splendid! Not only was the body of the stove silvered, but the pipe as well.

For several days we admired it before lighting a fire. When that day came, Mama, William, and I all participated, I with newspapers, William with kindling, Mama opening the damper and draft below, before applying the match. Then through the isinglass window in the door, the three of us watched the blaze increase and fill the body of our stove.

A scorched metallic stench began to permeate the room. In fascination the three of us saw a whitish blue-gray smoke ooze off the silvered heater. Wisps of smoke were starting at the bottom of the pipe and slowly crawling upward. Mama coughed.

"Open the doors, children, all of them! I'll get the windows. Oh, fiddlesticks, if I'd had the slightest notion——". She alternately coughed and sputtered as she flew about the room checking the damper, opening windows and fanning the smoke with newspapers. William and I grabbed papers and fanned, too.

The blue smoke continued to rise, and great silver blisters bubbled on the pipe and around the glistening belly of our stove. We saw the smoke creep along the ceiling of the room and finger its way stealthily around the door jamb into the hallway that led upstairs.

Suddenly there was a terrific thud which shook the chandelier in the living room and made it jangle. Even though I was coughing I could

49

hear Papa stumbling down the stairs.

There he stood, barefooted and in his nightshirt. His thick brown hair was tousled and his eyes looked strained.

"For Lord's sakes, Della," he shouted, "why didn't you consult me before you painted that thing?" He pointed at "the thing" with a far-flung gesture that took in the whole end of the room. "I could have told you what would happen."

"Now, Will," Mama said, fanning all the time, "there's no use talking about it."

I saw Papa open his mouth to object, but Mama didn't let him. "There's nothing you can do. You might just as well go back upstairs."

Papa gave a harassed look around the smoke-filled room, before his shirt tail disappeared into the hallway. In a minute there was a loud creak from above, then silence from upstairs.

It was only seven-thirty, and we knew that Papa had gone back to bed.

$\mathcal{M}$ore About Business

Papa was a good business man, and he liked to be with people. Endowed with a fine personality, he had the will to succeed in whatever he undertook, plus the capacity for planning, hard work and—Mama. Without any one of them he could never have progressed as he did. But it was Mama who counted the most when things looked blackest.

Soda Fountain

A few years after World War I, Papa had borrowed from the bank to pay a mortgage on some wheat land he owned. Business in general was so slow that many times during that year, he left the store in Mama's charge while he went out to walk or to talk to people simply because he couldn't stand to be inside with so little business.

That was when he decided to put in a soda fountain to stimulate trade. The store already had a popcorn machine near the front door where the tracked-in snow melted into little puddles on the red cement floor.

A group of popular high school boys used to stand in those puddles when they saw some newcomer about to enter from the cold. As he pushed open the door, they'd join hands, the last one reaching out for his, in greeting. It all seemed so friendly—and with those high school big shots too! But as prankster number one, with his feet in the water, touched the popcorn machine amid whoops of laughter from his co-horts, oscillating electric current carried their "welcoming" voltage

DELLA AND WILL GRAY, 1916

through the group to the shocked newcomer.

Apparently the pleasure of seeing their victims' discomfort or surprise far outweighed the comparable jolt experienced by them all.

When a salesman for fountain fixtures stayed with Papa until after midnight trying to make a sale, Papa saw his chance. After establishing a cash price of the fixtures they were dickering over, Papa said, "What are you going to give me for my popcorn machine?"

"Lord, Mr. Gray, I can't take that machine in on the deal. We have a dozen of those things now in our warehouse."

"That's all right with me," Papa said, "but let's get out of here. I'm tired, I want to get home." Papa got up to pull the cord that turned off the office light.

"Well, now wait a minute, Mr. Gray. You can see my position. Let's talk this over a little more."

Papa said there was no use keeping him up any longer if the popcorn machine didn't go in on the transaction. He wanted the fountain, but he couldn't afford it unless the machine was turned in.

Finally, it was agreed that the salesman would take the machine plus cash, which Papa had to borrow from the bank, and the Newstand would have a new soda fountain.

That fountain helped the store just about break even—but then only because Papa kept late hours to accommodate the picture show trade.

It was times like those when he'd say, "We'll never be able to send the children to college, Della. We'll never get enough ahead."

And Mama would say, "We've got to send them to college. They've got to go even if I have to get another job."

All this time she was the best salesperson Papa ever had. Besides keeping up her housework and devoting hours of time to the store, Mama provided us with recreation by reading to William and me or taking us on long Sunday walks. She told us stories, and helped us if we needed help in school. She couldn't have taken on another job, but the threat was enough to keep Papa working at schemes to get a little ahead, even if it meant starting another job. He did just that.

Saturday Night Dances

Papa leased the lodge hall over the brick corner grocery store. He hired three musicians to play for Saturday night dances during the summer months, and he sold tickets at the door. From holiday dances, like the 4th of July, the store netted about three hundred dollars a year, in fountain trade. Those dances pulled him out of the red.

While I was still a pre-teenager, Papa taught me to dance.

"Don't let your hand rest so heavily, Honey," he'd say if I let my arm sag. "That's better. Now you're dancing."

We'd circle the floor with a dip now and then to accent the graceful one-two-three of a waltz. Papa always whirled his partner effortlessly.

Mama was a good dancer too, but during the months that Papa leased the hall, she didn't dance much because of tending the store. After a dance, the whole family worked at the fountain.

"What would you like? Can I get something for you? Maltie as usual? Lemon or plain coke?" Dishes piled up and whoever had a minute found himself washing glasses and banana split dishes.

Papa worked faster than anybody. One night, in his hurry, he flung his arm back to reach a soda glass from behind the fountain and flipped Mama's nose glasses into the dish water.

"Just calm down, Mr. Gray," Mama said turning her back to the customers, "or you'll be working here without me." By the end of an eighteen hour day, they were both going on nervous energy.

To Buy Or Not To Buy

After the year when Papa avoided going into the red by leasing the dance hall, Gray's Newstand began making money. But on the advice of his banker, he borrowed to buy stock in the Wilbur Meat Company, plus more to pay the mortgage on some wheat land about 50 miles south of Wilbur.

A few years before, a stranger named Mr. Richardson had come into our Newstand and looked over our whole stock before buying the drug store across the street. That was when Papa felt forced to add perfumes, soaps and patent medicines to compete. Gray's Newstand now had everything but a pharmacy.

§⋆

"Mr. Gray, John and I want you and Mrs. Gray to go for a ride with us." It was Mrs. MacPherson, the banker's wife speaking to Papa in the store, in the mid 1920's.

"Thanks Mrs. Mac. Della can go, but I don't feel like leaving the store in charge of Jim." Jim Bolton was the boy who opened the store, worked after school and on weekends.

"No, we want you to come too. Jimmy will be perfectly all right with William and Helen to help him, and we won't be gone long."

That afternoon, Papa reluctantly left the business to go with Mama and the MacPhersons for a ride. After they had driven a short way, Mrs. MacPherson, riding in the back seat with Mama, said to Papa in the front seat, "Mr. Gray, why don't you and Mrs. Gray buy out Mr. Richardson?"

The idea was startling to both Papa and Mama. "There are just two reasons, Mrs. Mac. The first is that we already owe the bank money, as John here knows. The second is that in a couple of years we want to send the children to college, and we can't afford to take on any more obligations."

"Well, John and I think you should look into the possibilities, Mr. Gray."

For two weeks after that ride Papa lay awake nights mulling over the problems .

It would mean combining two complete stocks in a building no larger than the one we were in. It would mean borrowing a large sum of money and increasing the help. If the move were not successful, it would mean that Papa and Mama would be unable to send us both to college.

On the other side of the picture was the possibility of renting all of Elmer Larrick's building which housed both the drugstore and the post office behind. This would mean a much finer store than would otherwise be possible. By buying out Mr.Richardson, competition would be virtually eliminated, and if things went well, college would be assured.

First Papa went to the bank for further talk with Mr. Mac. Afterwards he talked to Mr. Larrick, the owner of the building in which the drugstore was housed. Finally he went to the drugstore owner, Mr. Richardson himself. Arrangements were drawn up for the drugstore stock to be bought by Papa at fifty cents on the dollar. Papa hadn't realized until then what a stiff competitor he had been.

With inventory completed, moving was begun. We all helped. As Mama and I washed and dried fountain glassware, it was carried across the street to the drugstore. Surplus fountain fixtures, inventory, and display cases were stored in the Hay building which for many years had been vacant.

In the meantime, the partition between the drugstore and the post office had been torn down. As blocks of mailboxes were carried out, merchandise and cases from the Newstand were brought in by the side door, and customers entered for business-as-usual by the front door. By midnight, Papa went to bed exhausted. Mama, William and I had gone to bed earlier.

Second Fire

About two o'clock one morning the whole town was awakened by the rising and falling wail of the fire siren. Papa and Mama jumped from bed to look out the window. The sky over the downtown section of Wilbur was an angry red. Flames could be seen licking the sky.

Mama ran down to the phone in the kitchen. Then she called as she came upstairs, "Will, it's the Hay building." By that time William and I were up and in Papa's and Mama's room looking out the window. Papa was dressed when Mama returned, white faced, from downstairs. Papa ran out the door to save his property stored in the Hay building.

When Mama, William and I arrived downtown, the streets were lined with townspeople. Some were in night clothes under coats, watching in fascination as the blankets of flame from the old Hay building billowed over the west wall. Flames were licking at the roof of the Thompson's Dry Goods store and the old Newstand. Husbands, fathers and brothers were fighting to save those adjoining buildings, though the fire in the Hay building was beyond control.

What started the fire was a smoldering cigarette. It was dropped by a volunteer carrying confetti, carnival supplies and concessions into the now-vacant Hay Building, for the upcoming "Jim Town Carnival."

When Saturday night dancers saw the fire, it was too late. Already flames which filled the inside of the building were breaking through the roof of the huge old building. Flaming red tongues licked the air and expanded into ballooning clouds of smoke against a slate-blue sky. The adjoining buildings, Thompson's Dry Goods and the Newstand were saved. Days later, smoldering embers left the south side of Main Street only a black pit filled with tortured ribs of iron at its center.

As for Papa, with the insurance money he repaid some of the bank loan early. The saving in interest meant—what else?—more money toward Papa's and Mama's goal: sending the twins to college!

Sweet Memories

As we grew older, William and I were often at the store. From an early age we learned to sell and make change for such things as postcards, newspapers, magazines, school supplies, chewing gum and candy. Later came fountain goods and even Columbia records, but Papa handled Kodak sales and he alone sold the Columbia Graphonolas (phonographs). Those he demonstrated in the area adjoining his office at the rear of the store. He'd had special compartments made for storing the dozens of records for potential customers' listening.

I especially liked being around Krause's Fine Chocolates. They came in shiny blue boxes which were shelved behind the candy display

W. P. Gray Newstand, Wilbur, Washington, 1926

Bert Denson behind chocolates; W. P. Gray beneath suspended sheet music.

cases. When their lids were lifted, the fragrance of chocolate tempted me to sample some of the delectable sweets—the caramels, the honeycomb chips, the nougats, the nut clusters and the marshmallow creams.

Like Eve I succumbed to temptation. Often when refilling the candy dishes inside the glass display cases, I surreptitiously gobbled chocolates as I made sure the fresh pieces were displayed at the front of the pressed glass plates and dishes, to insure selling the older chocolates first.

On top of the candy cases were penny candies in glass jars, packets of Sen-Sen for the breath, as well as horehound cough drops. Smith Brothers' Cough Drops, jaw breakers, gum and licorice were all there for the buying.

❧

Papa loved children and babies, and mothers loved to come into the store to show off their children and make a purchase from Mama while Papa held their babies and made over them.

If the store weren't busy, he'd spend as much time over a little kid's candy purchase as he would on a larger sale. One of his favorite stories involved little Jimmie.

One day little Jimmie came in and edged up to the candy counter where all the chocolate confections were neatly displayed inside. On top in tall jars were hard candies and nuts.

Jimmie pressed his nose against the glass and said, "How much is that?" indicating the first piece, within the case.

"Five cents." Papa told him.

He moved his nose a smidgen and pointed to the candy next to it. "How much is that?"

"Five cents."

"How much is that one?" pointing to the next piece.

"Five cents."

Jimmie went slowly down the whole line of candy until his eyes and finger indicated the very last one. "How much is that?"

"Five cents."

Jimmie looked up, dismay in his face. "Gee," he said, "Doncha have anything for a nickel?"

Inside Business

There were some years when Papa and Mama both looked tired and worried. Mama used to take a short nap in the afternoon before coming down to the store to relieve Papa while he went to the store's basement to rest. There was an iron cot down there, with a thin cotton mattress on it.

Often when he just couldn't stand staying in the store with only a trickle of business and several thousand dollars worth of goods on the shelves, Papa could relieve his feeling of frustration by talking politics outside. Politics took his mind off the business.

He could justify some of the frailties of the country's economics by the fact that the Democrats had been in power for seven years. Politics and baseball, during that time, probably served Papa as well as they can serve any man as an outlet from worry and the burdens of responsibility.

Because Papa continued advertising in *The Wilbur Register* in bad times as well as good, Walter Gillies, the editor, in appreciation, gave front page reports of Papa's baseball prowess every Thursday of the season.

"Gray's bunch of ball tossers proved too strong for Creston last Sunday. The local boys whaled the boys all over the entire park grounds in fierce shape and refused to be stopped at any stage. It's a shame the way Gray does do things when he's on the ball field. He displays no pity, whatever, be the opposing team strong or weak, and it is quite likely no more games will be secure from our neighbors on account of this trouncing."

Stories like that pleased Papa who liked to be considered a threat in either politics or baseball. But Papa didn't want to be taken for a sucker in any field, and in those days, if he suspected that he was being played for one, he was quick to flare up.

Those were the days when occasionally the big top circuses would come to town, bringing their clowns and animals, and beautiful painted ladies who rode on the heads of the elephants in the street parade. There were concession men, too.

During one such visit to the Newstand by a circus concessionaire, Papa insulted the man by telling him that if he didn't want to buy anything to get out. An argument followed, and the man invited Papa to "Take off them glasses and come outside if you wanna fight this out."

Papa was more than willing to meet the man on those terms. They walked out the door. As Papa reached up to remove his nose glasses and hand them to William, the fellow let loose with a terrific blow.

That was the end of the fight. Papa ended up in the street.

More Memories

Memorable Characters

At one time the "canary lady" lived not far from us. She intrigued me not just because it was said she had a house full of singing canaries, and we'd hear them sometimes when we passed by, but because of the fancy tent-like dress of sheer, black chiffon over the deep red satin dress beneath. It covered her round figure becomingly and was quite glamorous appearing as she padded about watering plants on her tiny porch in the mornings. She was the only woman I had ever seen who dressed in chiffon and silk before noon.

There were other memorable inhabitants of our small town. For instance, there was the grocery clerk in Hay's grocery department who, when asked the price of cantaloupe said with his usual twang, "Fifteen cents—two for thirty-five." I was young but better in math than he was, so I bought just one melon at a time when I did the shopping for Mama.

Mrs. Ring was a tall gaunt old lady always dressed in dark clothes, her straw hat anchored to the black scarf covering her hair. Every evening during spring, summer and into the fall, she made the rounds of some homes, getting "scraps for the chickens." She carried them home in a five-pound lard pail that swung from her arm. When our pie cherry tree was laden with fruit, or the sweet crab apple or yellow transparents were ripe, she enjoyed picking and eating them as she traded chit-chat with whomever was around. She often took fruit as well as her chicken scraps home. It was rumored she had lots of books in her weathered two-story house high on the hill with the chicken yard outside. I don't know how she existed in the cold weather; she was not a complainer, and each spring that I remember her coming to our back door, she looked just the same as she had the year before.

Nobody Fights Like the Gray Twins

Mama sometimes said, "Nobody fights like the Gray twins." I guess we did fight, but it was also true that, when observers ventured to side with either of us, we became as one against that ill-directed interference into our twinly goings-on. William could effectively anger me to the point of outrageous action with his teasing. He used his wits; I became emotional, which was just what he wanted!

One time when our parents left us alone at night, William said something that I resented. We ended up—he the pursued—racing through the kitchen, the living room and the hall again, until I pounced on him. Opening my mouth I bit him on the top of his head. The sound of shattered glass brought the awful realization that William's noggin had smashed the etched glass upper part of our heavy front door.

We both raced to the wall phone in the kitchen to call the lodge. Mama was called to the phone.

She had to leave her station among the sisterhood because the twins were calling. When she finally came to the phone, we both scrambled to be heard, but William grabbed the mouthpiece to tell his side of the story.

Mama's sternest voice said, "Get the glass off the floor right away. Put newspaper over the opening. Go to bed and don't call me again." The phone clicked.

I was indignant that she hadn't heard my version.

She really believed that nobody fights like the Gray twins. She always said it with such resigned conviction. But poor Mama, it must have been hard to be proven right so publicly.

The Cape

It was in the dry goods section of Hay's Department Store that Mama bought my coat with the cape. It was early fall, just the time when apples fell to the ground, and yellow poplar leaves curling under foot reminded us that Halloween was coming. We knew, too, that our cheeks would chap if we didn't dry them well after washing our faces.

When Mama and I pushed open the door and went into the store I spied the coat that I wanted, first thing. There it hung, on the rack, a lovely mustardy yellow one with a brown velvet collar and—a cape! Stitched under the velvet collar it hung down elbow-length all around.

I tried it on, and could hardly keep from dancing, I loved it so. Mama thought it very nice and, without consulting Papa, bought the coat. Parading into our store wearing it, I saw Papa scowl.

"What's that thing for?" The "thing" was the cape which he indicated with a nod of his head.

"It's a cape", I told him, fairly prancing with pleasure, "and it keeps me warmer than just a plain coat would. Look!" I spun around to make the cape fly out. "Isn't it pretty?"

But Papa didn't think so.

"That damned cape", he would mutter whenever he saw me wearing it. His aversion grew until finally he could stand it no more. I had it on in the store when he tightened his mouth decisively and reached resolutely into his pocket for his pocket knife.

"Come here, Helen", he said

When I reached Papa, standing in front of the candy counter, he turned up the brown, velvet collar, took hold of my beautiful cape, and with only a caution to hold still he began to cut. I felt the pull, I heard the ripping sound and I stood helpless. Then, with a yank, Papa severed the last threads and gave the cape a fling. I saw my lovely mustard colored cape land, like an ordinary rag, on the floor behind the counter!

Miserable, I ran crying to Mama.

"Oh, Will", she gasped, but there was no recourse. I could still wear the coat, but the cape was a thing of the past. She tried to comfort me.

She explained that Papa was upset much of the time, worried by the slump in business. Yet, here was a man who was so affectionate he would not leave the house to go just the few blocks to work without first kissing both his twins and our Mama goodbye.

Mama's Hair Pieces

I liked playing dress-up with the hair switches from Mama's dresser drawer. I'd sweep down the front hall stairs and into the living room, garbed in my finery from the rag bag in Mama's closet. I yearned to be an actress—like Shearer, for instance. She was so elegant.

The switches were fastened to my short braids and carefully arranged as the crowning glory to my transformation.

One afternoon when I was about ten, the doctor's wife, Mrs. Williams, who had very thin hair, came to call. She and Mama were having tea together when, creatively coifed and dressed, I glided before the captive audience.

When she saw my coiffure, the doctor's wife sighed in obvious admiration. "My," she said, "Helen will never have trouble fixing her hair." I smiled my thanks.

But suddenly I heard Mama saying, "If you'd like, Mrs. Williams, you may have one of the switches. I never use more than two." I wanted to protest. Happily, however, Mrs. Williams gracefully declined.

"Thank you, Mrs. Gray," she said, "but I have no talent for fixing hair." She touched the tiny knob of pulled-back hair and smiled ruefully.

Delighted that Mrs. Williams had turned down Mama's offer, I quickly exited with relief. With Mama's three switches, I could more easily pretend I was an actress—maybe like Norma Shearer.

Mama as Speaker

I used to watch Mama sitting at her golden oak desk writing letters or speeches. Her speeches had snatches of verse or appropriate quotations and she always received compliments afterwards. When the Eastern Star and Masonic lodges honored Papa and Mama on their golden wedding anniversary, *The Register* reported that Mama responded to the program "with a lovely talk and a most appropriate toast." Mama was never at a loss for just the right words graciously spoken.

Mama took great pride in the Wilbur Civic Club. Mrs. Farnsworth was the first president, and Mama next. She probably made more welcoming speeches to new teachers, for instance, than any other matron in town, at least when William and I were growing up. The club was disbanded in the 1930's, during the Depression years. When it was reorganized, Mama was president again.

One of their projects was to pay for orthopedic treatment for a child who was injured at birth. Mama wrote endless letters to the Children's Orthopedic Hospital in Seattle. She visited the home of the middle-aged parents to offer encouragement to them and their child. Once the club concerned itself with the medical care and help for a blind mother who was badly burned when her stove exploded. Mama used to walk across town to take food or clothing and to see that the patient was getting the medical care she needed. Other ladies did that, too, in our small town.

$\mathcal{L}$essons Learned

Mama often said that she regretted having never taught me the art of cooking and housekeeping before I left home. Oh, I could bake cakes, arrange flowers, broil steaks and slice tomatoes. But I had no interest in sewing, or being neat as a pin, or planning and preparing whole meals and doing housework.

The one time she depended on me to prepare at least one meal a day, was when she went to Missouri for a week's visit to her parents, who were not well. I was eleven or twelve.

Mama cooked a roast to serve us for several dinners; she left potatoes, salad vegetables, and a potato cake. I was to fix eggs and bacon with toast for breakfast. Papa could make suggestions as well as the coffee, but theoretically I was in charge of the kitchen.

The first night we had the roast warm. Dinner over, I put the roast back in the roaster and shoved it into the warming oven. The next night we sliced it cold, and I left it covered on top of the stove.

The following morning, since he came in to make coffee anyway, I left Papa to preside over breakfast. Afterwards I went outdoors to play baseball with the boys instead of doing my dishes. In the afternoon Papa needed me in the store after we had a milkshake and sandwich at the fountain for lunch.

That night we ate at the hotel because, as I told Papa, the kitchen wasn't very clean, and maybe I could help longer at the fountain if I didn't have to take time out to clean up the kitchen.

Result: food spoiled, and we ate at the fountain or at the hotel for the rest of Mama's visit. Obviously my education was inadequate in that area. Mama most often did these things herself. She found it less time-consuming than trying to convince a sometimes recalcitrant but otherwise satisfactory offspring of the joys gained by learning the fundamentals of everyday living.

॒॰

Some lessons in living are more readily acceptable from someone other than parents.

Even into high school I bit my nails. Nothing made me so aware of what an unbecoming habit it was until after our superintendent and his wife took in a more mature young man so he could finish high school. He never did seem like a high school student. He was reserved. One late afternoon, having just finished a hard game of tennis, I went to the store and he happened to be there. He looked at my red hands with the bitten nails, took one in his hand and said, "You really shouldn't bite your nails."

He seemed truly concerned. I knew he was right, and that marked the beginning of the real effort it took to break me of that miserable habit.

॒॰

Once, and only once, I told Mama to shut up. I was small and she was dry cleaning some clothes in the back yard. The cherry tree was in bloom and its fragrance mingled with the heavy odor of the solvent. Humming birds darted from the currant bushes to the trees. My mood didn't complement the beautiful day.

Mama scolded me for some offensive action, and with a sudden, terrible burst of independence I said, "Shut Up!"

She took her hands out of the tub, straightened up, and as she dried her hands on her apron, calmly but decisively said, "Go into the laundry room and shut the door, Helen. After you've had twenty minutes in which to think about this, I'll call you. Then you may come out."

All my independence gone, I marched into that 5'x 8' cell and stayed there. After what seemed an interminable period, Mama called

67

me. I walked meekly out, and with no objections I obediently followed her suggestion to "apologize and never do such a thing again."

Years later, in my mid-teens, I was again seized with a rebellious urge to express my displeasure verbally to Mama—but I didn't. I had reached the age where dramatic acting was wholeheartedly incorporated into my everyday life, and after a suggestion from her which I didn't take kindly, I turned, stalked majestically out of the kitchen, and as I reached the hall door, turned ever so slightly, and with a contemptuous toss of my head—I sneered.

I expected to be stopped with a word after my satisfying performance, or even to be yanked back into the kitchen, although mother had never done such a thing. Instead Mama just looked at me and then burst into tears. "I'll never forget that look as long as I live," Mama cried, "Oh, Helen, how could you do such a thing?"

I was a little frightened at what I had done. My fright was mingled with a sense of amazement. I ran to Mama and flung my arms about her. I told her that I was sorry and begged her to forgive me, assuring her that I hadn't meant to hurt her so.

But, somewhere inside of me, there welled up an almost wicked elation at the realization that I had been able to convey so much and elicit that remarkable response with just a look!

$\mathcal{L}$ife With Mama & Papa, Continued

William's Health

During our freshman year in high school, Mama was quarantined with William for scarlet fever. Papa had a room at the Madsen Hotel, where the two of us ate our meals. I slept at an elderly neighbor's home. Tennis practice after school, and evening rehearsals as an accompanist for the high school operettas, kept me too busy to worry about my twin's condition or Mama's burden at home. For me, I was adapting to the drama of life's uncertainties, and as a teenager I loved it.

From our preschool years William had suffered from chronic appendicitis. Mama always feared the outcome of an operation, so whenever an attack occurred, he would be put to bed with an ice pack on the pain. The doctor stopped in daily during these attacks.

It was during our high school years that William had gone to Spokane with Papa on a buying trip. They had left immediately after school to return the next night.

That night when the telephone rang insistently, I dashed in to answer it.

"Hello, two-five? Spokane is calling Mrs. Gray." It was the operator.

"Hello—yes." Mama heard Papa's voice on the other end of the line. "Oh, no. What time did they operate? Is he all right? You'll stay with him, Will?" It was a statement in the form of a question.

She turned from the wall phone. "It's William," she said. "He was operated on for appendicitis late this afternoon. He just came out from under the ether. To think he had to go through that without my being there. I've always been afraid for him to go through an operation. I didn't know about it, and now it's all over. Maybe it's just as well."

It was. From then on William began to slowly catch up with me and would finally exceed my height in college.

Detente—William and Dad

Until William and I were fourteen or fifteen we were content to call our parents "Papa and Mama." Then we noticed how many of our friends called their parents "Mother and Dad." Consequently we soon shared the conviction that "Mama and Papa" sounded much too juvenile for persons of our maturity.

"Mother" easily supplanted "Mama" in our vocabularies. To me "Daddy" came naturally. William's choices, however, were "Dad", "Daddy" or "Father." Since the latter suggested the ministerial type it was never given consideration. "Daddy" was deemed sissified for a boy. William chose "Dad."

It was an unfortunate choice. Papa termed the designation disrespectful; he forbade his son to call him that. William decided to address Papa with "hey" if he wanted his attention. He refused to revert to the affectionate term of our childhood. We were too old for that. Papa had given him no choice. The gauntlet was thrown down.

For a long time William might simply clear his throat to attract attention. Or he'd say, "Uh—hey—uh" with a sliding inflection. That was so Papa would assume he was thinking so hard about the matter to be presented that the omission of a proper salutation was unpremeditated. But the matter finally came to a head in the drugstore when we were nearing sixteen.

It was on an afternoon when Papa was checking goods at the back of the drugstore. William, waiting on a customer, needed a price. Disdaining to shout "Papa" or "Father," William cleared his throat, held the article up for Papa to see and called, "Hey-uh-Dad."

No answer.

William realized that the word "Dad" had probably displeased Papa. He also knew that he was not going to revert to "Papa" again after a stand-off of nearly eighteen months.

Papa scowled. "Are you talking to me, William?"

"Uh—yes."

"If you can't address me properly, don't address me at all!"

"I just wanted to know how much this is," William called back.

"Well, how do you ask?"

My twin looked at his customer then at the box in his hand. "Could you tell me this price?" He held it up for Papa to see.

There was a harsh silence while Papa digested the fact that he could never compel his son to call him "Daddy," or "Father," or even "Papa" again. "Thirty-five cents," he said and went back to his work.

Gradually, Papa recognized that William seldom called him anything anymore. Slowly he began to overlook the number of times that "Dad" slipped out when William talked. Finally he responded to "Dad" as calmly as he had when William and I both called him "Papa" those many years before.

In a way it was like a mediation agreement. Only there was no mediator and no agreement. They both just quit pushing and it all came about quite naturally.

Papa Gets a Car

For years, after cars became a common mode of transportation and an instrument of pleasure, Papa refused to have one. We children pleaded with him to get one so that we could be among those whose fathers could furnish rides to school, weenie roasts, and parties in the country. Other families went riding on Sunday afternoons and took trips to Spokane in their cars, while we had to depend on their invitations to be able to enjoy such pleasures.

But Papa was adamant. "They're just an unnecessary expense, and we don't need one. I don't want my family riding all over the country

71

anyway." And that settled it.

Then radios were invented, and there seemed to be a good market for them. Papa cautiously studied the situation before deciding to handle the Zenith. After borrowing the necessary money, and as business developed, Papa worked night and day installing aerials for his customers, and demonstrating the radio's wonders.

A wheat farmer took Papa and a large console model to his farm for a demonstration. He worked putting up the aerial, showing the man the intricacies of tuning squawks out, and satisfying the customer of the enjoyment the instrument would bring him. The man offered to give Papa $85 in cash plus a Ford coupe valued at $100, in exchange for the radio.

The deal was made. Late that night Papa chugged over the country roads and into town in a car with no lights—and no assurance that if he stopped he could start again. He abandoned it in front of McCarthy's Ford garage and walked home. But late the following afternoon, when Papa came home for dinner, you can imagine our delighted surprise to see him driving up to the house in a car! Even though it was only an old second-hand Ford coupe, we dashed out excitedly to meet him.

"If a man's going to sell radios he's got to have a car in order to make demonstrations and deliveries," Papa explained, and William and I certainly agreed with him!

Challenges

Mama's determination that William and I have a college education motivated our facing up to any challenges that came. Competition was an important part of the learning process in our school. Blackboard contests between grades at the primary level helped us learn to add, subtract, divide and multiply quickly. We were our own computers in those days.

Reading aloud, spelling drills and written tests were part of the tools used by our teachers to help us learn the basics of education. At the end of our eighth grade, William passed the required State exams in geography, spelling, history and arithmetic with a score of 98, third highest in the state!

Josephine Corliss Preston, State Superintendent of Public Instruction, wrote him a letter of congratulation. He responded with a thank you note. Mama made sure we did that when appropriate. Later, Mrs. Preston stopped in the store while touring eastern Washington, "to meet William and his family." She seemed to have a special spot in her heart for him.

Algebra

I don't think William needed help with any scholastic challenges, but nothing had ever prepared me for algebra.

One day I came tearing into the house after school, "I hate it, I hate it! I can't do those old problems! I don't understand them and I never will!"

Mama calmly asked me to sit beside her at the library table, so called because it had book shelves at each end. Reluctantly, I sat. After a while we were working together going over every step necessary to solve the offending problems. Suddenly, the light dawned and I got it! And it was all due to Mama. She knew how to handle this teenager rebelling against spending time on something for which she saw not the slightest use.

I must confess that algebra is again largely a mystery to me. But now, thank goodness, it doesn't matter.

The Performing Arts

When a traveling production company put on a Tom Thumb Wedding to make money for some good cause, I'd experienced my first taste of acting in public, at age five. I was cast as the mother of the bride—not the usual kind—I had to sing "Oh Promise Me". No one else in that age category was available.

In the second grade I was old Nicomus, Hiawatha's mother. Though it was only pantomime, I was proud to be in the cast. After a high school play in which I played the sweet young heroine, the coach told Mama that everyone commented on my performance. Never, even when the Collie puppy, substituting for the called-for "lap-dog", waddled to the front of the stage and piddled, did I forsake my role. The fluffy scene stealer broke up the rest of the cast and much of the audience, but not me. I took acting seriously; I remained "in character" like, well, a real actress would have done.

Dance

Mama arranged for my dancing lessons from an English lady, who commuted weekly from Spokane for just one summer. The class learned the Highland Fling and the Dance of the Hours. In the latter, I flitted about tapping the other Hours, who waited for me to activate them. But the most challenging dance, which might be either a solo or ensemble number, was the Scarf Dance. The one specific requirement was a veil made of two yards of thin, pale blue, 48-inch material attached to our little fingers with brass rings. I think the teacher's idea was to teach us how to handle such a prop. It was not easy for ten and eleven year olds. Getting it to float as we danced was a little like hoisting a kite without enough wind. I doubt that our teacher envisioned our performing in public with it, but I did. My debut that summer was doing the Highland Fling on the school yard lawn at the reception for our departing superintendent and his wife, the McCormacks. I would conclude my part in the program with the challenging Scarf Dance.

Unfortunately, in the first number I stopped flinging four measures before the recorded music did. Probably only a true Scotsman would have cared, but in mortification I rebelled against reappearing as a dancer. Papa, however, either knew instinctively that The Show Must Go On, or he wanted to take a picture. Anyway, he tapped on the window of the basement sewing room, where I was fretting in my white dress and white Keds, and with my blue veil.

He motioned me to come out PDQ—an aphorism the family jokingly used when action was desired, only this time Papa wasn't joking. I obeyed, but the snapshot taken, as I solemnly arabesqued toward his faithful Kodak, clearly indicated that my rendition lacked the ethereal quality that a Scarf Dance really deserved.

Perhaps that explains why, ten years later, in my first year with the Whitman College Glee Club, I politely declined to be one of the dancers in an activities dance (tennis, football, etc.) during the spring concert. Unfortunately, Director Howard Pratt had previously given the projected program to the scribe for the yearbook, the Waiilatpu. There I received undeserved credit for a dance I never performed. Ah, me. Of such mistakes false fame is sometimes born.

Innocents Abroad

The April afternoon that the announcement was made to the seventh and eighth grades that tryouts for a County Declamation Contest were to be held, I went home bubbling over with the news that I wanted to be in it. The final contest was to be in May at Davenport, the county seat. Mama, who was often called upon to make speeches, was most cooperative. Papa said, "Well, if Helen's to do it, get the best teacher available."

After some inquiries around school, Mama engaged the Domestic Science teacher. She had studied elocution.

My piece was from Mark Twain's *Innocents Abroad*. It challenged my imagination and reinforced my ever-present urge to act.

I practiced on Mama at home. Papa, at the store, was spared. William conveniently disappeared whenever I started. At school, the fifth, sixth, seventh and eighth grades acted as my practice audience. They didn't mind. It meant nearly fifteen minutes away from the 3-R's.

By May, I was letter perfect.

As we walked back to the house where I was supposed to rest before dressing for the contest, my stomach ached from excitement and hot weather—or possibly from the ice cream soda that had topped off a bad restaurant dinner. Relaxation was impossible. Finally Mama allowed me to dress for the contest.

Then I thought of William's warning. "You better be good. I'm paying a substitute 20 cents to deliver my papers."

Josephine Simas declaimed before I did. Her acting convinced me that she was the one to beat. Besides, her dress was more elegant than mine and she had beautiful ringlets and a huge hair bow too, but mine was bigger and I had pink garters. The garters were my idea.

Afterwards, someone played the piano below stage. The school principal came out. He praised all the contestants, thanked the audience for coming, cleared his throat and announced the winners in reverse order.

"The bronze medal for third place," he began as he named a boy, of whose performance I have no recollection. "And to the seventh grade contestant from Sprague..." It was the girl with the curls who stepped daintily forward to accept the silver medal as the crowd clapped its approval.

"And to the seventh grade contestant from Wilbur goes the gold medal as winner of first place." My first gold—I still have it!

After the last awards, friends and relatives converged on the contestants to congratulate them. William's freckled face was grinning. "Nice going, Twinny," he said.

He'd gotten his twenty cents worth.

Declamation Contests

An unforgettable growing-up day for me was the day of the Lincoln County High School track meet. I was a sophomore. I would once again represent our school in the Declamation contest.

I learned a lot after that Saturday. During the day our tennis team, of which I was a member, had won the tennis pennant. A gold medal was also mine for accuracy in typing. Wilbur's Debate Team was given the season's championship pennant; I had been on that team, as well. But best of all came in the evening. With my declamation came another gold. To win that, I became an actress and I reveled in it!

Monday morning I went to school buoyant, happy not only for our teams' awards but especially for that second gold medal. I looked forward to having my friends share that joy with me.

Not one girl even mentioned the meet! I was crushed; I suffered silently.

That night Mama heard me sobbing. She came into the bedroom. Tearfully I showed her the lone entry in the diary which I envisioned as the chronicle for all future tragedies of my life.

"Honors are empty if one has no friends."

Predictably she helped me understand the vagaries of human nature, and I returned to school, outwardly unscathed, the next day.

And the diary? It disappeared someplace.

I never was very neat.

William's Triumph

William had previously won top medal for an essay on Lincoln, and he had performed great characterizations for school plays. He regularly held class offices. He was student body officer and basketball manager when the team won the county championship. He edited the school newspaper *The Sage* and outside of school hours worked for *The Wilbur Register.*

Capping it all was his performance in *"The Murderer's Confession"*

78

by Edgar Allen Poe.

I volunteered to be his coach. Experience, you know.

After my dismissal as his mentor, Mama took William to Spokane twice for elocution lessons. His rendition was fine tuned into a harrowing tale told with chilling restraint by William as a mad man. He spoke with deadened tone and the cunning inflection of a crazed creature tormented by visions of an eye—the eye of a murdered man—always on him. His hands shook; his eyes darted craftily about; he moved stealthily.

In reporting the results of the contest, the Davenport paper headlined the following piece with:

WILLIAM GRAY WINS DECLAMATORY CONTEST
Decision of the Judges Approved by the Audience
The announcement of the decision of the judges
which carried with it an award of first place was
greeted with applause which did not cease until
William Gray arose and bowed his appreciation.

It was a triumph, and I was proud that he was my twin!

Music

For William and me, high school days were filled with activities, both in school and out. I was continuing piano lessons. Mrs. McCormack was my first teacher. Then Mrs. Williams, the doctor's wife. But none compared to Josephine Clark, who demanded much and gave much to those under her instruction.

One of her assignments was that I play five or six unfamiliar hymns daily, in absolutely strict time. That was to facilitate sight reading, and it proved a great social asset in later years, when many of our parties centered around singing new tunes at the piano.

One of Mrs. Clark's recitals was in the theater, complete with flowers and silver achievement cups. Once she even staged a play. I was in it. It was called *Not So Sharp in A Flat* or something like that.

In the mid-twenties several of her more advanced music students accompanied Mrs. Clark to Spokane to hear the great Paderewski in concert. I was among them.

As one encore, Paderewski played the Minute Waltz, in the allotted time. Mrs. Clark gave me the opportunity to emulate that feat during my junior year of high school, after the Whitman Glee Club sang in our school gymnasium. She hosted a soirée honoring Director Howard Pratt and several Glee Club members whom he chose to bring.

Classmates Dean Arbogast, Charlotte Jurginsen and I were included, ostensibly to entertain with demonstrations of virtuosity. Dean and Charlotte were superb.

I remember going to the piano, my hands clammy with excitement, settling myself, and then beginning with speed and clarity. Before I had gone very far I had struck a vacuum. For some seconds my fingers kept repeating the same measures, like a broken record. All at once I visualized the last half page of the piece and, with merciful ease, proceeded to tear that off in record time.

My rendition must have embarrassed Mrs. Clark. It did me. Despite that I had a wonderful time; for when refreshments were served, Gordon Boles, a handsome Whitman senior, monopolized my time for the rest of the evening.

To a teenager that was success!

William's Musical Challenge

The drug store was directly across from the bank on Main Street and to the east of our former Newstand. It was in 1926 that it became the W. P. Gray Drug Store. Years later, in a 1938 full-page ad of appreciation, Papa would recount the situation:

We were not druggists nor did we have the capital to buy the business, but we did have the encouragement and backing of friends. This support has continued throughout the years and for this we are grateful.

The evening he and Mama had the grand opening of the Drugstore, Papa wanted it to be a memorable one. So besides the usual treats for customers and visitors, he arranged for a musical program to begin at 9:00 p.m.

A piano was borrowed for the occasion, and Papa had insisted that William play a clarinet solo. I accompanied him. In dread anticipation of the occasion we practiced dutifully at home.

On opening night the place looked like a florist shop. Beribboned bouquets from wholesalers were all over the place. The piano was in the center of the long store.

During the piano introduction, William stood with his clarinet in hand, moistening his dry lips and fingering the keys of his instrument. Then he raised the clarinet to play. How he felt toward Papa, who was responsible for his being there, I can only guess. I was thinking not only of Papa but of the people who had to listen. At least William tried to do something about it. He stopped after the first few notes.

"Guess I better tune up." He grinned and his audience laughed with him.

I hit an "A". With difficulty he tried to force the clarinet's tone up as we began again. The dissonance still persisted. The piano and woodwind on that memorable occasion were just about a half a tone apart.

Finally the clarinet emitted a heart rendering squawk and my troubled twin gave up. "Ah heck," he announced, "I can't play. The thing's flat!"

The experience didn't blight his life permanently, but from then on his repertoire consisted of about eight measures of "Mood Indigo" on the piano.

❧

In 1926, no longer sold were sheet music, records and Columbia Graphonolas (phonographs), nor were radios, which the Newstand had carried for awhile. Papa had even bought a second-hand car for delivery purposes. Now two pharmacists, Roseville pottery, Fostoria glassware and jewelry were all part of the change.

Missing from the newly purchased W. P. Gray Drug Store were the two round ice cream tables and the eight chairs that had graced the front part of the Newstand. Mama took the chairs home to use at the kitchen table. The pressed glass dishes that had held Krause's chocolates were stored in the basement of the Drug Store.

Mama was president of the new corporation; our full-time pharmacist, who had bought into the business, was vice-president; Papa was secretary-treasurer. Both William and I waited on customers.

$\mathcal{P}$apa and Politics

Mama didn't like Papa's devotion to politics. She used to threaten not to go near the store if Papa didn't tend to business and not leave it all to her, us children and the druggist.

"Will," she'd say, "sometimes the fountain is packed, and there'll be two or three other customers waiting to be waited on, while you have your head practically on top of some man telling him how you think the country should be run. I wish you'd think how this store should be run instead."

At the end of the month he and Mama would make out the statements, while William and I folded them, putting them into two accordion-like holders. On the first of each month, Papa would take one folder and start collecting from the business houses he had allowed to charge, and from customers who were in arrears in their payments, whom he might meet on the street. William took the easier ones to collect, which might be twice as many, but he'd be through before Papa was well started, because Papa couldn't forget politics. We'd see him standing in front of the bank, or the meat market or the hardware store, talking confidentially to some poor fellow who probably couldn't break away.

If the other person tried to agree with him and illustrate Papa's point with a story of his own, the man would be interrupted with, "That's just what I tell these fellows. We've got to have a high tariff to protect our interests. I tell you, if the Democrats get in they're going to find this country will go to the dogs."

If it was a Democrat he happened to be talking to, Papa's voice got louder when they tried to interrupt, and he'd cut them off with "My God, man!" He got very worked up over politics. "Now you listen to me. Look at the statistics."

Not everyone agreed with Papa.

§.

After Papa decided to buy out the drugstore in 1926, he announced to the Republican leaders in his district that he would have to withdraw from his first political race for State Representative. He did it regretfully, but he knew that he wouldn't have time to campaign the five-county district with all the work involved in taking inventory, moving, and running more than twice as large a business as before.

Despite Mama's disapproval, but because of the insistence of the Republicans, and their promise to work for him, Papa consented to stay in the race. Of course, Papa never would have done it if he really hadn't deep down inside wanted to.

But, true to his promise to Mama, he saw to it that business came first, and he made only three campaign trips.

William and I typed and stuffed envelopes for the campaign. As high school debater, I went with Papa on two trips, listening to him rehearse his speech of the evening as he drove.

Papa was at his best talking confidentially to one or two people. Then his intimate presentation of his political views were usually very convincing. But, when he talked from a platform he had difficulty getting away from that same soft, rapid presentation.

While he rehearsed at the wheel, I'd interrupt him with, "Open your mouth more, Daddy, and enunciate better. People won't be able to understand you." And Papa would rehearse some more.

On those trips he always introduced me as "my campaign manager", and people seemed to like the fact that he was a proud family man.

In 1926 he won his race for State Representative. Two years later he began the first of three terms as State Senator.

Mama went to Olympia only infrequently while Papa was in the legislature. That would be for a few days to accompany Papa to a legis-lative or inaugural ball.

$\mathcal{F}$arewell to
Wilbur High School

You may recall that during one of our high school years, William had accompanied Papa on a buying trip to Spokane and was rushed to the Deaconess Hospital there, to have his appendix removed.

As a result of his absence from the final test in one of his subjects, the teacher gave him "D" for the quarter. That kept him from being class valedictorian. The family didn't like it; the principal didn't like it; it seemed unfair, but that didn't change the matter.

I was given the title of valedictorian and delivered the valedictory address. But that didn't alter the fact that I was really only "Pretender to the Throne."

Lilacs in baskets were at the edge of the stage and on the piano below. At center stage was the table with our diplomas jacketed in red leather and stamped with gold. School board members and the superintendent sat at one side of our two rows of chairs arranged in a gentle arc. The new red velvet curtains presented by our class hung in heavy folds at either side of the stage. An almost reverent feeling permeated the auditorium and I felt beautiful and pure and loving.

Finally my name was called. I stepped center front and began the valedictory. Our class motto was "Character is the Only True Diploma." It was also the title and subject of my speech. The speech was filled with quotations like *What doth it profit a man if he gain the whole world yet lose his own soul?* It ended with a fourteen line poem.

The Wilbur Register printed my address in its entirety after describing it as—*the most popular number on the program—short, well delivered and filled with good thoughts.*

In retrospect, it seems quite obvious that there wasn't much room left for any original thinking!

On Class Day when William read his class prophecy and received his letter awards for athletic manager and declamation, I received letters for tennis and debate and contributed a class song.

In the true tradition of class songs, ours, written to the tune of "What Does It Matter?", ended with:

> "Life was never one sweet song
> Things are liable to go wrong
> Wilbur High School, we'll remember you
> And the joys so true
> So—
> What Does It Matter?
> Yeah, Wilbur!"

Years later, in writing of William's journalistic career, *The Wilbur Register* listed his valedictorianship as an early accomplishment. I'm sure no one questioned it for a minute. He really was, in the accepted understanding of the term, the brightest in the class.

Being listed as salutatorian didn't bother him. He knew what he wanted to do with his life and was already on course.

That year Papa had offered him his diamond solitaire if he wouldn't smoke until he was twenty-one. William thanked Papa but said he'd rather have a typewriter, now, to take to college in the fall. His goal was to become a journalist.

The typewriter was ordered immediately. William never did smoke, and his success as a journalist would far surpass any expectations ever envisioned during our teenage years in Wilbur.

Mama said that when we were two and a half or three years old, she noticed one day that William seemed uncomfortable in the new shoes he was wearing. "Honey," she asked, "Does your shoe hurt?" She knelt to feel his little boot.

"No," he admitted, "but my foot does."

Such precision later served him well in that chosen field of journalism.

Choosing A College

Our parents' goal of a college education for William and me was well on its way to being realized. As high school valedictorian and salutatorian we were automatically offered scholarships from the State College of Washington (now Washington State University at Pullman). I wanted to attend Whitman College—"Yale of the Northwest" according to Mrs. Sadie Goffinett, our foreign language teacher. Whitman was in the New England-type-town of Walla Walla in southeast Washington. William, who was already a part-time journalist on the local paper, had favored the University of Washington. Since Whitman was small, Mama and Papa favored it as our starting place even though the tuition was $500 for each of us. That was no small amount in 1927. William agreed to go to Whitman for our freshman year.

For years we had been banking our allowances, and any money that came our way, toward college. Papa and Mama had succeeded in their efforts, so the following September, our applications to Whitman having been accepted, William and I were ready to go. His new typewriter and my new trunk were there when we boarded the train.

Afterwards, Mama said people used to ask her, "Didn't it break your heart to send both children off to college at once?"

She never hesitated to answer, "That's something we've always wanted—to send the children to college. I'm not going to cry now."

How wise that, during the summer months of our teen years, Papa had supplemented income from the store, with receipts from Saturday night dances. Adults and teenagers alike did their own thing to "Barney Google", "It Ain't Gonna Rain No More", "Three O'clock in the Morning",

"Who's Sorry Now?" and "Always".

"Always" still reminds me of the tennis player from Davenport, whom I really didn't know, but of whom I was very much aware, since he was the top man on his school's tennis squad and I played on the Wilbur team. One night the phone rang. When I answered, Hugh identified himself and asked if he could come to the house. Of course he could.

Hugh and his younger brother, also a tennis player, showed up. We spent the evening singing at the piano, with William playing clarinet or drums, and Mama enjoying it all. And all because Hugh brought me a piece of sheet music that I still have. It was "Always", one of the pieces played when Papa taught me to whirl, dip, and glide at those Saturday night dances.

Later as a freshman at Whitman's All-College dances, I thrilled every time Clarence Monroe, a senior, led me onto the floor to whirl, dip and glide, just the way Papa had taught me in the lodge hall above the grocery store in Wilbur.

College

Sororities & Fraternities

I listened carefully when offered advice by Marion Alexander, the boy on whom I'd had a crush for years. I wonder if he even knew how much I liked him. Now a fraternity man at Washington State College and with two sisters in Theta, he advised that if their sisterhood was not on the Whitman campus, "Pledge Kappa Kappa Gamma." I made a mental note of that. Theta was not there.

Within the first few weeks of school, William, who would transfer to the University of Washington for his Sophomore year, pledged a fraternity and withdrew, was courted by other fraternities, but wisely deferred until he was on the Seattle campus.

Induction, Latin

Even though our campus was small, William and I seldom saw each other. Life was so busy. I became a Kappa pledge, was cast as the romantic lead in A. S. Milne's *The Butter and Egg Man* and was on the verge of flunking Latin, all before going home for Christmas.

Latin was a requirement at Whitman. I'd had two years of high school Latin, so was registered for Latin II. After having forgotten most of what I'd learned, I asked lots of questions of the young teacher, whose reading of the ancient tongue was sheer poetry. That is, I asked questions until the one day I approached him to buy a ticket to a college play at the

Keylor Grand theater.

"I'll buy *two*, Miss Gray, if you'll go with me." He sort of blurted it out.

For a moment I was speechless. That was unheard of in Wilbur, a coed going out with a college teacher!

I didn't know how to answer. He was young, boyishly good looking, and was said to have been spurned the year before by a high school senior from the local St. Paul's Episcopal Girls' School. She had cruelly thrown his ring from the back of the departing train, as he stood watching her leave.

I must have sold him the tickets and accepted. All I remember of the whole affair is that he was a perfect gentleman, but I was so embarrassed, having gone out with a teacher, that from that time on, I never, never again asked a question in Latin II, seldom looked up, ended up with five hours of "D" in the course and couldn't be initiated with the rest of my pledge class. I should have asked my older sorority sisters for advice before committing myself to that date, but group living was new to me. Trying to be independent instead of learning from those with more experience, I learned the hard way.

Facts of Life

One day my roommate Ruth Thomson and I were asked by an older Kappa sister to meet with a doctor's daughter for a little talk. It seems we were a source of mortification to our chosen group because of the questions we asked in biology—also a required course. Elizabeth Patterson, a junior and a doctor's daughter, was designated the one to explain to my roomie Ruth and me the facts of reproduction, which our parents had apparently neglected to be specific about.

Ruth and William had exchanged pictures. His was on her dressing table. From that time on Ruth turned his face to the wall whenever she disrobed. As for me, I learned that babies didn't come as a result of sitting on a boy's lap the wrong way. It was good to have that cleared up.

Dame Fashion

One of the nice things about a small college in a relatively small town is that the college is contacted for talent on special occasions.

During my sophomore year, Mrs. Davis, the drama teacher, called me to her office to say Montgomery Ward asked for a student to act as MC for a fashion show. It would be a paying job, no amount was mentioned. I said I'd like to do it. I set my fee at $15 a night with $5 for an accompanist. I wanted to open the show with a musical reading—*Dame Fashion*. Offer accepted.

I enjoyed looking over the fashions—sometimes coining descriptive phrases like "angel crepe" to describe a heavenly pink evening dress.

The first show was in the local movie theater on a Wednesday night. We traveled to Pullman the following Wednesday and to Moscow, Idaho, the Wednesday after—both college towns.

I missed psychology class both days, a pattern I couldn't afford to continue. Shortly after that a letter came from Montgomery Ward headquarters asking me to MC shows across the country.

Mama's and Papa's goal of a college education for the twins made the decision an easy one. Our goal mirrored theirs. I declined with thanks.

Chicago

My goal in choosing Whitman had been to go with its glee club on their annual tour throughout the Northwest. When I'd been in high school and the club had performed in Wilbur, Ilabelle Shanahan was featured in a musical reading. I wanted to emulate her in that role of featured entertainer.

For years I'd adapted popular songs and material from *The Etude* or songs such as "Mighty Like A Rose" as musical readings—speaking some of the words, singing bits of the lyrics to dramatize them in my own way, so I felt that my goal was not unrealistic.

About my singing voice I had no illusions. High notes scared me, so I took singing lessons at the Conservatory for two years. Then at the end of my sophomore year, when Director Howard Pratt offered the opportunity for students to accompany him for five or six weeks of summer studies at the Bush Conservatory in Chicago, I signed up without telling Papa or Mama. I had previously arranged, however, to borrow four hundred dollars from Kappa's national headquarters. The college agreed to let me do kitchen chores beginning in the fall in exchange for board. Papa and Mama were happy to reimburse my Kappa loan with monthly payments equivalent to their usual payment to the college. And so things all worked out. My horizons were broadening.

In Chicago I studied acting under Elias Day, who directed the plays performed on the Chautauqua circuits during the summer months. Under his wife Oranne Truitt Day, I gained a new repertoire of both musical and other readings.

Nearing A Goal

Following the summer studies in Chicago with Mr. Pratt and five or six other conservatory students, Beverly Means, newly graduated and a member of the group, returned to Wilbur with me. She had signed a teaching contract with the Wilbur School Board and she agreed to appear in concert with me before school opened there. It was a good way to become known to the townspeople. She had an unusual contralto voice and good stage presence. I would accompany her. My part of the program consisted of readings and pianologues. The proceeds would go to pay part of my debt to Kappa.

For both of us, it was successful. My debt was reduced by over $100.00. Beverly eventually married Sigvard Hansen, one of the handsomest and best liked young men in town.

Preparing for that evening of entertainment gave me a repertoire, and I could readily accept a summons from Mr. Pratt to be part of the program for a lodge convention in Walla Walla, shortly after school started that fall.

The following day, as I walked past his glass-doored studio, he beckoned me to enter. He told me that I was to go on the glee club tour that year. I played it cool. I mentioned that I'd planned on turning out for the drama club play. I don't think I fooled him one bit, since I'd tried out for glee club for two years and hadn't made it. Now as a junior, when told that I would also entertain at high school assemblies the afternoons of the concerts, my delight must have been apparent.

Toward the close of my junior year I called Mama one night. I was dejected, disillusioned, even though having just been chosen as sorority president for the coming year. I'm not sure that I told Mama the real reason for my low spirits, but an incoming junior and fine violinist was going to represent our Kappa chapter at the national convention the coming summer. I had hoped to go. I think I was jealous. It was like a defeat, and inwardly I wasn't a very good sport about it all. But only Mama might have surmised that, for only in the telephone booth did I lose the usual independent, good-natured mien that came naturally.

Mama let me tell her that I wanted to join William at the University of Washington in the fall, that I didn't enjoy Whitman anymore. But Mama took the wind out of my sails. She offered no objections. Amazed, I decided to rethink the idea.

Within a few weeks, coeds from town and from Prentiss Hall gathered in the courtyard behind the hall to watch the solemn procession of senior Mortar Board women. In their caps and gowns they wended their way among onlookers to tap, with a rose, the outstanding junior girls who would carry on the traditions of the honorary the next year. I was tapped by one of my sorority sisters and joined the procession.

Love and Other Problems

The summer following my junior year in college, I went to Yellowstone Park. A sorority sister was returning for her second summer. We worked up some numbers together because college employees were entertainers after the chores were done.

I waited tables at Lake Yellowstone Lodge and, like several other romantics, fell in love.

The object of my affection was from Salt Lake City. He had been offered, under the aegis of United States Senator Smoot of Utah, the opportunity to prepare himself for a career in the field of diplomacy. He had turned it down. Although he had a sister at home, he felt that his mother

needed his presence. Apparently his father, a successful engineer, was gone much of the time, and I gathered that a drinking problem alienated him from the Mormon family. Even though our family backgrounds were so different, Jack was the first man who seemed like the one I wanted to have as a real part of my future. We corresponded regularly during the ensuing year.

One day, a letter came addressed to the Housemother of Kappa Kappa Gamma. Individual sororities and Independents, all housed in Prentiss, had no individual housemothers. Instead, Prentiss Hall housed the one housemother and dean of women, both of whom were available to all girls. Consequently, Jack's letter from Utah was given to me, as president of KKG. It contained a dollar bill with which to buy one hundred votes for Helen Gray, at a penny a vote. I was one of the nominees for May queen. The two highest vote getters would have their pictures sent to a Hollywood luminary for judging.

I know now that I was guilty of misappropriation of funds when I used his money to pay for something other than votes, but the enormity of my crime was lost on me at the time.

When I thanked Jack, I confessed that, with no illusions as to my beauty or even popularity, I'd thought, "Why waste the money?" and used it to help pay for a brown and beige print dress.

The girl who I thought would win, apparently fell short of Hollywood's standards of beauty and, like me, was an attendant to the chosen queen, who fulfilled her duties beautifully.

94

Glee Club and Spokane

My final year at Whitman was a rewarding one. I was assured of a place with the glee club again, with the role of the Cookie Witch in a shortened version of Humperdinck's *Hansel and Gretel* to climax the evening program

The Walla Walla Union praised individual performers and the overall production, also citing Dan Elam, who played the father, and me, as examples of "Whitman's outstanding dramatic talent." Unlike Dan, who had a magnificent voice, I vocally interpreted, in my talk-and/or-sing style, the villainess of the piece—while covering the stage on my broomstick and glorying in the juicy meal anticipated. This had delighted the State Penitentiary inmates at our tryout performance there; they loved to cheer the "bad guys".

The part of Hansel was played by young Edward P. Morgan, later a noted radio commentator. He was also in A. S. Milne's *The Truth About Blayds,* in which I had the female lead. Playing opposite me was Albert Garretson, later a Rhodes scholar, legal advisor to Hailie Selassie of Ethiopia, and then in confidential work for the United States Government in London.

That production was invited to play in Spokane under the aegis of the Spokane Little Theater. I suffered throat trouble for two days before the show. I think it was psychological for it was fine on the big night.

Among the audience were Grandma Green, visiting from Missouri, and Mama. Grandma and I had our picture taken together the next morning. She was holding a large bouquet. I don't know whether the flowers were hers or mine, but she deserved all the love and appreciation that her family bestowed upon her.

College Recap

At Whitman for four years, besides starring in drama productions and touring as featured performer with the Glee Club, I'd been honored with memberships in Arrows—sophomore honorary, Mortar Board in my junior year, and President of the Dramatic Club as a senior. I graduated as president of my sorority.

No one envisioned the paths which William's career would take after high school, a year at Whitman, then four years at the University of Washington with a major in journalism. There he was fast proving his talent as a journalist with a fine sense of humor, coupled with good judgment and good taste. These qualities became evident in his senior year editorship of *Columns*, the University humor magazine, and enabled him to remain editor his full term. This had not been the fate of a preceding editor or two. A member of Phi Kappa Sigma fraternity, he was elected to Sigma Delta Chi journalistic honorary besides receiving other recognition by peers or faculty. A distinguished future was ahead.

William graduated from the University of Washington in 1932, a year after I'd received my diploma from Whitman College. Too many journalism grads were working in service stations or not at all. Papa wanted to buy *The Register* for William to ensure his safety from such an experience. But William declined with proper gratitude and thanks. He wanted to stay in Seattle where the chances of making big contacts in the world of journalists weren't so remote.

My invitation to his graduation came in the following letter:

WILLIAM P. GRAY, JR.   CLARENCE J. WINBERG
Editor   Business Manager

UNIVERSITY OF WASHINGTON
COLUMNS
114 COMMERCE HALL
SEATTLE
Monday 16 May

Miss Helen Gray
Teacher—

Please for you to come over here to Seattle to spend the week of June third to thirteenth with me. It will be oh what fun. Canoeing, swimming, boating, movies, beach parties, sunshine, hearts and flowers, all courtesy Seattle Chamber of

Commerce. Why don't you attend summer school here? Board and room very cheap, and the campus most attractive.

Anyway, please spend as much of that week here as you can. You owe it to yourself and your brother. And I'll guarantee you'll love it. Remember, it's our last week in college, and it wouldn't even be that if I hadn't lasted a year too long.

Shucks, you couldn't do otherwise.

With my love,
William

I joined the family to see him graduate.

$\mathcal{T}he$ Real World

Parlez-Vous Français?

Before graduation, while the country was still depressed economically, I had signed a contract to teach high school in Marcus, a small town not far from Colville, in northeastern Washington, and near the Canadian border. The brick school building, housed both grade and high school students. Superintendent McAlexander headed the staff of four teachers for the eight lower grades, and four of us who taught at the high school level.

For ninety-five dollars a month I was to teach girls chorus, three classes of English, one of French (which I hadn't had since high school), and one botany class. In that class some smart students tried to catch me up by asking what kind of seeds "these brown things are?" I rightly guessed they were sheep droppings, though botany was not my forte; nor was French, but I was lucky there.

My landlady was a little Scotswoman, married to a jolly little English baker. Her Scottish parents lived in a cottage behind the King house, in which I had a room. Mrs. King told me of a lady in Marcus who had grown up in a Quebec convent while speaking only French until she was twenty. Said lady was bright, independent, had read a great deal about the history of the Catholic Church, and had cancer. She burned bread to make charcoal, for she'd read that was good for her affliction. Her loyalty to the Church had eroded, but she told me that when she knew she was going to die, she would embrace its rituals again.

98

The lady agreed to help me with my French. Every evening I visited her with my French book and questions. She'd check my translations, and pronunciation. She approved my French translation of "Where the Blue of the Night Meets the Gold of the Day," which the students and I crooned together in class.

Whether any Parisian Frenchman could have understood our Quebec French, I have no way of knowing, but during our second year of class work, my mentor dropped in and elicited conversation with the students by questioning them in French. In the next issue of the weekly paper was a letter commending Miss Gray's class on their ability to communicate in French. When passing through France twenty-five years later, I found that the natives talked so fast I understood barely a word. So much for my high school French!

Fini Love

After my first year of teaching, Jack came from Utah to visit and meet the family in Wilbur. Doubts began to fill my mind, but I promised to go to Salt Lake City for a week of Christmas vacation.

Our family was particular about keeping teeth in repair. Jack's large cavity in the front of his mouth offended me, but I lacked the courage to tell him.

Was money the problem? Could I live without feeling financially secure? My pay as a newly licensed teacher was sometimes uncashable in the 1930's. I could not support two of us, nor did I want to. A trip to Salt Lake City for a week of Christmas vacation answered my question.

That visit, enjoyable in many ways, made me realize that I could never marry Jack, but I hoped we would remain friends. It didn't work out that way. After confessing my change of heart in a letter, I naively hoped for understanding and forgiveness, if that was what was called for. My letter was never answered.

Senator Gray's Farm-to-Market Bill

Papa was proud of his accomplishments and recognition as a law maker. Seattle political writer M. M. Mattison wrote:

"Senator W. P. Gray, Wilbur Republican has taught senate lawyers to respect 'cow county' leadership more highly. Gray had a bill exempting automobile owners from liability for accidents occurring to guest passengers. The judiciary committee unanimously condemned it. Gray saved it from indefinite postponement by suggesting an amendment. It came back, again condemned, and once more he over-rode the lawyers, then fought and saved it.

"Gray is a lanky interior merchant born in Astoria, Oregon where the wild waves grow."

Perhaps he was suggesting that Papa made waves; I like to think so. The home town weekly also approved of Papa's ability to get results. *The Wilbur Register* related the following as—"a story illustrating the effectiveness of practical politics."

"During Langlie's first term as governor he made a non-political trip around the state in an off-election year. His schedule included a luncheon in the old American Legion Hall in Wilbur after a morning appearance in Odessa.

"A number of Wilburites attended the Odessa meeting and escorted the governor to Wilbur for the luncheon. Senator Gray, an advocate of good highways and farm-to-market roads had the privilege of driving the Governor between the two towns.

"At that time the highway between Odessa and Wilbur was graveled and Gray was pushing to have it oiled.

"Bill Gray saw to it that his car was near the end of the caravan and took dead aim for all the chuck holes and washboard ruts, all the time explaining that the highway needed to be improved and oiled. The dust billowing up from the cars ahead and the rough ride apparently had the desired effect. It wasn't long before the highway was much improved."

Papa liked to add that Governor Langlie signed his Farm-to-Market bill the following session of the legislature.

Happy Happenstance

The happenstance that was to completely change my life had occurred that summer of 1932, on a trip to Spokane with Papa.

We were in the lobby of the Davenport Hotel, famous for its live music from the balcony, its liquid sounds from real birds, and the fragrance of fresh flowers at the base of the fountain, its splashing waters making music of its own.

That was where Papa and the contender for the Democratic Party's nomination for Governor, recognized one another. Papa introduced me to Clarence D. Martin, wealthy mill owner from Cheney. His secretary, was the sister-in-law of my superintendent.

Superintendent Grant McAlexander had called his teachers in at the end of our first year, before contract signing . Because of the district's financial condition, we were asked to take a salary cut of five dollars a month. That was understandable. Some months our warrants could not be cashed. In fact Papa had cashed one of mine once when I wanted a new coat.

It was upon learning later that McAlexander had convinced the school board to tack our surrendered dollars onto his paycheck that I knew that I did not want to be working under such a man.

None of this was relayed to the future governor, but I did tell him that I was excited about being able to vote for the first time in a gubernatorial election. I would vote *against* the incumbent Republican governor, because his loyalty to his wife was questionable, I explained. However, if he, Mr. Martin, were again his party's nominee, he could be assured of my vote. (Ironically, after he became governor, his marks for conjugal fidelity were no higher than his predecessor's.)

Came September. As I walked back to school one noon hour, a convertible with its top down pulled up. On the passenger side sat Clarence D. Martin. Driving was Harry Huse, later head of the State Department of Licenses. They edged to the curb to say they were on their way to Colville

to campaign. Would I like to go with them? I answered the facetious question with, "Thanks, but..." Classes awaited me.

After that I didn't see Clarence D. Martin until the night of his Inaugural Ball in January of 1932, when Mama and I both went to Olympia for the occasion.

We shopped in the afternoon. With long white gloves and pearls, Mama wore a black satin gown cut on the bias. Around her shoulders she wore a white *crêpe de Chine* scarf with wide fringes of silver lace at each end.

My black crepe sheath had a wide belt of brilliant bugle beads sewn diagonally at the hipline. My black velvet evening jacket was also bought for the occasion. Its detachable white fur collar was flattering, and before we left the hotel room, I could tell by Papa's response that he was proud of his two ladies.

When the new Governor twice asked me to dance, I felt conspicuously honored. When he took me to my seat, he proposed that Papa bring me, with Mama, of course, on Sunday morning for a tour of the executive offices, with lunch afterwards at the mansion.

I expressed my regrets. My scheduled departure by train to Spokane, then a bus to Marcus, precluded that. I had to get back to teach.

Governor Martin asked who my superintendent was, said he knew him and for Papa to bring me to the office in the morning, and he'd fix it up.

When we appeared, several men were with Governor Martin. After introductions were made, he asked, "Can you take shorthand?" I said I could, and he dictated the following telegram:

SUPERINTENDENT GRANT MCALEXANDER
MARCUS, WASHINGTON
    WE, THE UNDERSIGNED, ASSUME FULL RESPONSIBILITY FOR
MISS GRAY'S ABSENCE OF HALF A DAY MONDAY. STOP. SEND US THE
BILL.

CLARENCE D. MARTIN
R. T. HARGREAVES
N. D. SHOWALTER
W. P. GRAY

Quite an impressive list of signatures. Besides the governor, Dr. Hargreaves was head of Cheney Normal School (later Eastern Washington College of Education). Dr. Showalter was the State Superintendent of Public Instruction, and Papa was Senator representing three counties.

The wire was sent immediately. That afternoon Governor Martin offered me a job in his office.

Upon my return to Marcus, I told the head of the school board that I would not be teaching the following year, that I had another commitment. I delighted in swearing him to secrecy, for I didn't want my superintendent to know until the matter of new contracts came up in the spring. I wanted him to be surprised and, hopefully, disappointed that he hadn't been the first to know.

Directing (and creating) Drama

In the meantime, that spring, I welcomed the opportunity to direct the senior class play. It was not easy selling the idea to the most capable girl in class that a character role was the plum, the one that people would remember. It was difficult casting the role of ingenue, the role the girls thought most desirable; none seemed to possess the special quality which makes the love element compelling. Rehearsal hours were limited;

some of the cast were dependent on school buses. But it worked out. After the one performance of our non-royalty show, Dr. Dimmit, visiting High School Supervisor from Olympia, came backstage to tell us that over the state he had seen the same play five times in the last few weeks—and that ours was the best.

I was pleased, but the superintendent was not. I had appeared before the opening curtain to give credits and to name the cast—thus saving the cost of printed programs, I said. But I had not cleared with him.

Maybe the news of his taking me down a notch backstage for such presumptuous behavior became fodder for talk among students riding the school buses. At least the last paragraph of the following letter seemed to offer that as a clue. The letter was from the mother of Bobbie Sandoz, an unforgettable, vivacious sophomore student who rode the bus.

The letter arrived in Wilbur about two weeks before I left for the change and excitement of a new career, new friends, and social contacts that were to welcome me. The letter read:

My dear Miss Gray,

I am so sorry that I did not get to talk with you yesterday before you left. You were busy with Mrs. Stevens when I first saw you, and later when I looked for you, you had gone for good.

I want you to know, Miss Gray, that I wish you all happiness and success in your new position and I know that you will have many more advantages than you had at Marcus.

When you think of us up here once in awhile, think of me too, won't you? And if you are ever up this way again call on us, please.

I also want you to know how very much credit I think you deserve for the senior play last Friday evening. You, alone, deserve the credit for that play's success and no one knows it better than I do.

Sincerely,
Sandy

104

And then her perky daughter added:

PS. "Them there's my sentiments, too."—Bobbie

Footnote: Mrs. Stevens (mentioned in the above letter) was the plump and loving young farm wife and mother of two little boys. The younger cherub loved to "say pieces." Mrs. Stevens insisted on making me a full-sized sunflower boy and girl quilt when I declined to be paid for the joy of bringing new little pieces for him to learn, and for the pleasure of hearing him "perform" for his mother and me. Several years later a Colville news release told of the death of a farmer when the tractor he was driving rolled on a hill, pinning him beneath. It was Mr. Stevens, the proud, devoted and hard working head of one of the happiest families I can remember. Their possessions were few, but the home atmosphere radiated contentment. I loved them all, the father and the now widowed mother and her two fatherless boys.

ℳarriages

Between 1931 and 1933 I taught, before becoming receptionist in the office of Governor Clarence D. Martin in Olympia, from June to October. It was there in our capitol city that I met my future husband, Ian Wesley Christopher.

Chet Dawson, a yachtsman from Seattle, said he wanted me to meet a couple of brothers, Ian and Elmon Christopher, who were outstanding sailors from the Olympia Yacht Club—but that he didn't want me to like them too much. Chet had indi-cated that he liked me, when he and his sister brought me to Olympia after I was a guest in their home, en route from Wilbur to my new job. Their father Senator Dawson and Papa were friends, serving to-gether in the legislature.

IAN WESLEY CHRISTOPHER
ABOUT 1933, AT 33 YEARS OF AGE.

I was attracted to Ian the minute he looked up and smiled, all in sailing whites with his cap tipped jauntily to one side. His impressive vocabulary and the fact that he was then active in civic affairs added to the attraction. And he bought me a water lily corsage. How original, I thought.

Within the week, Ian had introduced me to sailing in his 31 foot sloop, Galatea, and I was wearing his fraternity pin. Five and a half months later, Ian and I were married in Wilbur.

Ian was of Norwegian stock. His grandparents had brought four sons to this country in the mid-1800's. A daughter and then their youngest son, Albert H. Christopher, were born in America.

Ian's mother, Maude Chapman, was courted by Albert who rode by bicycle from Seattle to Sellwood, out of Portland, Oregon, to win her hand.

Both sides of that family had business backgrounds. The following, from the obituary of Ian's father, is just a partial list of the array of his activities in the community, from the diversity of a bicycle shop in Seattle to once owning and managing the magnificent Opera House in Olympia.

"Albert H. Christopher, 63, for the past 40 years had been intimately identified with the growth and progress of Olympia. Mr. Christopher's first business contact was as a real estate dealer. Three additions of Olympia—Summit and Evergreen parks and Main Street addition—were platted by him.

"Mr. Christopher always stood for the things that made for a better society. He was for a number of years a director of the YMCA, was school director several years, serving in that capacity when the school was built.

"He was also on the building committee of the Elks lodge when their temple was constructed. He was a trustee of the Olympia Golf and Country Club during the construction of the course and club house at Butler's Cove."

I would like to have known the man, but he died before I came to Olympia.

My twin and I would each find ourselves drawn to a lifelong mate of Norwegian decent.

William, after graduating, worked for the Seattle Star, began freelance work for Time magazine, and fell in love with Fredrika Ryland. Freddy was the daughter of a Seattle attorney and his wife, both prominent in the Norwegian community.

Freddy was my sole attendant, and Elmon was Ian's, when Ian Wesley Christopher and I married in the home I grew up in, on December 2, 1933.

For some reason, I had a bias against ostentatious weddings. I didn't even invite the Governor. He let me know he felt slighted. The marriage certificate misspelled Marguerite, my middle name. Despite all this, it was legal, and Ian and I are still married after—at last count— 63 years.

On the eve of Mama and Papa's 30th wedding anniversary, December 25, 1934, William married Fredrika Ryland.

Four months after their wedding, our first child, James Gray Christopher, was born April 26, 1935.

The following epistle arrived from his newly-married uncle, William P. Gray, Jr., when he heard of the coming event:

Dear Helen and Ian:

The accompanying happy thoughts (Think Each Day A Happy Thought) are put down with the hope that you will find time to sing them to the prodigious germ on nights when the waiting seems hard.

To you, expectant father, we wish as merry a session of floor pacing as the hospital has ever witnessed. We recommend strict training for this event, and stout shoes and aspirin.

To you, expectant mother, we recommend the competitive spirit. Pick another woman in similar straits and suggest a race. Happy Delivery!

Love and Diapers, William P. Jr. (Uncle)

The accompanying thoughts, with appropriate illustrations surrounding William's unpublished verse, were enclosed:

Lullaby Written to Exert a Pre-Natal Influence
on My Embryonic Nephew

Lullaby! Prodigious germ!
Fruit of human cravings,
Let your Mama rest—don't squirm—
List to Uncle's ravings:
Life is just a sucker's snare
(Consult most any poet)
But fish that bite are never rare—
Sanger! Freud! We know it:

Love, libido, aspirin,
Epsom salts and brandy—
One thing's sure, potential one:
This life holds more than candy.

Your tender skin will please the folks,
They'll think your feet are dandy;
In later years (I tell no jokes)
You'll find some Lifebuoy handy.

Sleep while you may, my tiny bud,
Time will soon be flying
Toward insomnia, marriage, doubt—
All plagues, all rest-defying.

Lullaby! Blest cynosure!
(Papa's ginger caused thee.)
Life is just a sucker's lure.
I pass on thoughts that haunt me.

L'Envoi

And if a girl child, let her squall—
Teeth and colic come to all.

                                    W.P.G., Jr.

Papa and Politics, Continued

In 1934, two years after Roosevelt's presidential victory and the Democratic landslide, Mama's worries over Papa in politics were solved effortlessly. After eight years in the Legislature—one term as Representative and three terms as Senator—Papa was defeated.

"It's just as well, Will," Mama comforted him, "Now you can spend more time on the business."

Aside from Papa's time spent on business and local civic matters, he would then—and in decades to come—serve many organizations whose causes he felt were worthwhile. During World War II he headed Government bond drives for Lincoln County. He attended State Good Roads Association meetings, served on the executive committee of the Columbia Basin Development League, and raised funds for the Republican Party.

A *Wilbur Register* article from the early '30's closed with:

> "He has interested himself in more civic affairs than perhaps any other person in the community. He has donated liberally of his time and ability to more worth-while causes than any other person we might think of. Of course, there are those who disagree with him on many things, but everyone will admit that he gets things done when he sets out to do them. Such a man is invaluable in any community.

"His business ability is recognized in the healthy condition of the town's finances, and yet during his administration as mayor, there have been many municipal improvements."

PHOTO BY WILSON MANTOR
Mayor W. P. Gray

Papa's final years in politics were crowned by the ten years that he served as Mayor of Wilbur. While he didn't enjoy complaints about somebody's chickens getting into somebody else's yard, he did enjoy the attendant mayoral duties that kept the small town on the map.

The following speech, by Papa, broadcast over Spokane's radio KFPY in 1939 expressed the pride he felt in the town whose development over the years he had so tirelessly fostered:

"As mayor of the lively town of Wilbur, I am happy to extend greetings this afternoon to our radio listeners.

"Wilbur is a town with several distinct claims to fame. Wilbur gave Washington one of its governors, the late Marion E. Hay. This was the home of the man who inspired Fathers' Day, the late William J. Smart, father of Mrs. John Brace Dodd of Spokane.

"Wilbur is the gateway to the Poil valley and large mineral and timber lands to the north. The Colville Indian Agency at Nespelum has its outlet through Wilbur. Roads lead into Wilbur from all directions and it is a shopping center for a large area.

"Ours is the first small town in the Big Bend to build its own outdoor swimming pool. Wilbur has a fine school and its athletic teams have brought home many championships. Wilbur claims the finest race track for a small town in the northwest, and one of the liveliest annual race meets anywhere.

"We have a fine public park for which we must give a great deal of credit to the Women's Civic Club. Wilbur has an abundance of fine spring water, a public library, a golf course, modern business houses, no indebtedness, a low tax rate, and best of all, a splendid civic spirit.

"And while Wilbur cannot call Grand Coulee its very own project, Wilbur is proud to be known as the eastern gateway to the dam.

"Wilbur is a complete town, alive to the present, doing things and looking to the future. Among the industries and business activities, we find our people engaged in wheat growing, warehousing and storing this important crop. The town stations and garages. It is a gasoline and oil distribution center for a large area.

"Wilbur boasts numerous fine grocery and meat shops, clothing, variety, department and furniture stores. Here is located a large telephone office which is the toll center for all calls west. Wilbur has a district office for electric distribution over a wide area.

"Lawyers, doctors, druggists, ministers, teachers and a dentist make a large professional group in the town. We have a modern hotel and restaurants. Two funeral homes, a laundry, tailor and dry cleaning establishments, modern beauty and barber shops complete the long list of enterprises in which our people are engaged. Several new homes and business buildings have recently been built.

"Soon or late, frequently or only occasionally, Wilbur expects to see you, and welcomes you as I do this afternoon by radio.

"Our thanks go to the sponsors of this broadcast, which we hope you have enjoyed."

Papa initially served eight years as Mayor before retiring from that office. Though urged to run again, he declined.

The following 1942 letter to C.F. and Zane D. Cosby, the father-son publisher/editor of the local paper, adds insight into Papa's character:

The Wilbur Register
Cosby & Cosby, Editors
Wilbur, Washington

Dear Sirs:

I just want you to know that I am very grateful to the Wilbur Register for the many fine things they have said of my efforts in a public way since it has become known that I wish to be relieved of the responsibility of the duties as Mayor of

Wilbur. Having been connected in various public enterprises, City and otherwise, it is indeed a great satisfaction to feel that in a measure the efforts made have met with some approval. While being human as we all are, mistakes have and will be made, and I fully realize that I have made them. A motto which hung in the office of one of my early employers has always lingered in my memory. It said:

He who makes no mistakes does nothing
He who makes too many loses his job.

The motto was hung on the wall of the office of former Governor M. E. Hay where his employees could at all times view it. My efforts have always been to give my best efforts and trusting that there would not be TOO MANY MISTAKES.

Very sincerely,
W. P. Gray

P. S. This letter is not intended for publication, it is in appreciation of the things you have said in my behalf.
Again thanks,
W. P. G.

Near the end of the four-year respite which followed, he and Mama flew to New York to see William honored by the Press Club of America for his distinguished work as a foreign war correspondent for TIME magazine during World War II.

Upon their return to Wilbur, Mama and Papa learned that in their absence, despite having refused to run, Papa was elected mayor again.

In the March 10, 1949 issue of *The Wilbur Register* the following information appeared. It tells, better than I can, the part Papa played in serving his town and state.

"Perhaps no one in Wilbur is so widely known as W. P. 'Bill' Gray. His civic and public activities—past and present

—have acquainted him with persons and sections of the entire state.

"Bill became prominent in state politics in 1926 when he was elected to the state house of representatives. In 1928 he began service as a state senator, serving until 1934, during four sessions of the Senate. After returning from Olympia, he was elected mayor of Wilbur, a post he held for 10 years. After a four-year breathing spell he was again elected mayor last fall and is devoting a lot of his time as head of our city government.

"His civic activities cover many fields. He found time to manage all eight of the horse race meets sponsored by the Wilbur Commercial Club; he managed the Wilbur Fair in earlier days; took an active part in promoting and financing the Wilbur swimming pool; managed the pool for seven years after its completion; and managed the Wilbur baseball team for the same number of years after he quit playing (Bill estimates that he was active in the sport for some 30 years.)

"He served as county chairman of the bond drives during World War II; filled the office of Commercial Club president several terms; is past Master of the Masons; a member of the Shrine; has been Worthy Patron of the Eastern Star lodge at various times; and was the first Daddy Advisor of the Rainbow Girls Assembly."

Papa was so proud of being chosen by the girls themselves as their advisor.

Drafted, he served the town he loved, but halfway through that third term, he asked to be relieved of the responsibility. His energy and drive were no longer that of a younger man. And a possible trip to New York to visit William, Fredrika, and their three children, Margrethe (born the same year as Sonja), Larry (the same year as Gretchen) and Bruce (same year as Billy) appealed to him and to Mama.

Could Papa Be Ill?

I was aware that Papa was walking with a cane beginning in the mid-1950's. But when we were together, his spirits seemed good; he spent some time in his office, kept track of his few investments, did appraisals for the state and felt secure in his family's love. But having given up the position of mayor, he no longer had the challenges, the recognition that he had enjoyed as an important public figure.

His legs bothered him some, so he drove his Oldsmobile wherever he went. There was no regular exercise, and Mama confided in William that Papa's failing memory concerned her. William understood the need humans have for continuing love and appreciation, to ward off fears that sometimes come when the days of active involvement are of necessity lessened.

In response to Mama's letter of November 1955, described by William as memory problems and "your worries about his worries, and what to do about this whole problem," William wrote:

"I wish I had the right answer, but since I don't have anything but some ideas and hunches we'll have to work with those.

"My first hunch is that Dad has always worried quite a lot, and that in his late 70's this lifetime tendency tends to focus on fewer things, as his interests diminish, and therefore to intensify. In other words, years ago he could scatter his worries over a broad field of activity, and no single worry got big enough to be very disturbing: he could worry at the same time about the store, about the Republican campaign, the local legislature, the Good Roads Association, about putting the kids through college, about baseball, about real estate, about the Commercial Club and so on. Any number of things kept his mind busy. Now he is down to fewer interests— namely, his stocks, his appraisals and, most of all, his own well-being as age comes on.

116

"He can get terribly worried, and even imagine all kinds of dire things (such as getting 'fired' from his State job as Appraiser), and these concentrated worries tend to depress him. They probably leave him in a state where he indeed doesn't quite think straight—his mind at 77 is probably tired, there should be some way for it to relax. Maybe nature takes part in this process—makes people forget in order to relieve them of a load.

"A doctor friend tells me that anybody like Dad, who still *can* worry about losing his grip, hasn't gone too far in the process of aging or senility. Later it may come to the point, in any person with this tendency, where he is *not aware* of his loss of sharpness. So let us assume that Dad is still in pretty *good* shape—simply because he is still sharp enough to worry about it. I think maybe you should *reassure* him on that point, whenever he shows some fright. If he *knows* that he is still doing pretty well, considering his age, in fact is in *average condition or better* for a man of his age, then he will quit worrying so much about that. That's the first step. 'Accentuate the positive', as Bing Crosby said. It will make you both feel better.

"I read a news item recently which stressed the need for 'love and gentle care' in cases where an elderly person shows senility. I repeat that I think that Dad is far from any real difficulty, but to prevent it you have the best remedy in your own daily contacts with him. At this age, he wants the security of knowing he is loved and respected, that he has you and his home and the love of his family. He is a very sensitive man, actually—I remember an occasion in Olympia, when both Helen and I were in town with him, when he broke down and wept like a child because we had chosen to go out on dates instead of going to a legislative function with him. He feels slights, or imagines them. It is necessary to understand this, as I'm sure you do better than I, in thinking about what seems

117

to be his current problem. If he is kept happy, if he can be reassured that he is all right, it will be the best possible medicine.

"A man's ego is a terrible problem—it needs constant massaging—and when it is no longer flattered by election to office or appointment to the work given younger men, then it must be flattered by wives and children. Probably Helen and I could help by writing more often, and directing special ideas to Dad, and I'll try to do my part.

"Frankly, I take after Dad. I am a worrier too, and I worry now that I'll be just like Dad—forgetful and fearful of it—at an earlier age than he. Last week I had some strain here at the office. I thought an ambitious young executive from Time Life was trying to take over some of my editorial authority. I worried myself into a minor depression for some days, and sent him a cable. I worried more when no reply came from him. Finally I got an apologetic reply, saying he was sorry for his inept wording of the memo. I had worried unnecessarily, and I'm sure Dad does this much of the time. But I swear my own dark suspicions were like Dad's. And he'll be less forgetful when he is through worrying.

"Now I know that people can become problems for themselves and others, as age comes on, and if that really happens there will be time to worry about it. But Dad sounds fine on the telephone, and he seemed to be still a very healthy man this summer—too preoccupied with little worries, to be sure, but still able to worry, which is more important. So let's try to keep him cheerful with the assurance that a little forgetfulness is normal, that he's still as much loved and respected as ever, that he has done a great job in his life and still has a lot of television shows to look at. (William and I had given them a TV for their 50th wedding anniversary.)

"And furthermore that you should both fly east next spring again.

Love, *Bill*"

$\widehat{\mathcal{M}}ainly$ About William

A perfect time for Papa and Mama to make a trip to the Big Apple had been when William, president of the Overseas Press Club of America, 1952–1953, was to be honored by that organization in 1953.

William had served as a correspondent in the Pacific and Philippines during World War II. In New York he became editor of the International Editions of LIFE magazine. He was instrumental in organizing a staff from 10 Latin American countries and the United States to produce the Spanish language edition of LIFE for distribution in Mexico, the Caribbean, South America and Spain.

In the public service scene, William had served as president of the Purchase Board of Education and the University of Washington Alumni Club in New York. I'm still amazed. I don't know how he had time to serve them.

The night that he was honored, William's name appeared only as Vice President of the Overseas Press Club of America's Correspondents Fund and as Chairman of the Dinner Committee.

The Overseas Press Club of America's Correspondents Fund, according to the program, "is established to provide relief for men and women who have served the American Press and Radio abroad and where necessary to aid the families of those who have given their lives."

Our parents' goals, of an education for William and me, were achieved in Wilbur and in the college and university halls of learning. Yet

WILLIAM AS A CORRESPONDENT
IN CHINA AFTER WWII

WILLIAM AS LIFE
INTERNATIONAL'S EDITOR

as the speaker enumerated the characteristics with which William brought his goals to reality—and for which he was being honored that night—Mama and Papa recognized that these were the characteristics of their own lives and the personality of the town in which they'd raised us.

Closing Speech by J. Clifford Stark, OPC Dinner, May 12, 1953

"The administration of Bill Gray as President of the Overseas Press Club will always be a memorable one in the history of the Club. For years, its members have realized that the Club could never become the vital force in international journalism of which it is capable, without a home suitable as a center for an expanded program of activities and useful service.

"Even before he became President, Bill Gray began for-mulating some practical plans to translate this desire into reality. It required money, in sizable amounts. But this did not daunt him. As President, he carried these plans forward and developed a program of action. Another equally important desire of the Club was to find a suitable way to honor the heroes of the American press—some members of the Club and some not—who gave their lives abroad in the service of a free American press.

"Bill Gray saw the possibility of accomplishing both of these objectives through a Memorial Fund Drive. There were some skeptics who cast doubt upon the generosity of the American press, American business, and the American public at large in supporting such a worthy purpose—not Bill Gray. With the help of other members of the Club who shared his confidence and courage, he organized and launched a Memorial Fund Drive, with results which you have heard tonight. Even before the drive started, he further displayed his confidence by taking an option on a building to become this Memorial Press Center. The building now is paid for, awaiting remodeling and furnishing, and we hope that by September or October of this year, the Overseas Press Club will be established in its new home.

"The Club is indebted to Bill Gray for the leadership, the faith and perseverance which are making this possible. As a small token of the appreciation of the Overseas Press Club to you, Bill Gray, for your outstanding contribution, and of the esteem and affection in which you are held by your fellow members, I take pleasure in presenting to you this plaque, inscribed as follows:

TO
WILLIAM P. GRAY
PRESIDENT 1952–53

FOR DISTINGUISHED SERVICES TO THIS CLUB
IN BRINGING TO REALITY ITS DREAM
OF A MEMORIAL CENTER
HONORING HEROES OF THE AMERICAN PRESS.

Transitions

For over fifty years my mother and father had shared a truly fine marriage. She was proud of him; he of her, and they took pride in their children. Shortly before his death, as he rested on the davenport while recuperating from the flu, he murmured, "I'm all washed up now." It was said with the despair which comes to people who have been active all their lives and find illness hard to accept.

Two days later he was shaving when the attack came. While in the kitchen, Mama heard a thud from the room above. She raced upstairs in time to hear Papa call her name and then, "Put me on my bed."

Despite the efforts of the doctor and the inhalator squad, my father died.

The obituary said he died of congestive heart failure. I believe he was ready.

I think he wanted it that way.

After Papa's death, February, 1957, William, now Editor of LIFE International, flew from New York and I drove from Olympia, to be with Mama.

Now, as a wife and mother of two boys, James Gray and William Ian, and two girls, Sonja Lee and Gretchen Diane, I thought sadly that our children would never again feel the strength of their grandfather's personality, nor admire his tremendous convictions about his country's affairs, or laugh with him as he joked. Offsetting that was relief in knowing that the man who had served both his community and state so well had gone swiftly when Death called.

A few days later my feelings of joy yet sorrow, happiness but pain, expressed themselves as I sat at the piano. I wrote them down.

Thoughts on Losing One's Father

Odd —
Having lost in death
Our father so beloved
in life,
I feel myself impelled to sing
again.

Quickly death came
The mind not robbed of faculties,
No lengthy suffering endured
by him.

Alas, our father's gone.
His grandchildren will never know
The warmth of his great gentleness
again.

And yet
Having lost in death
Him whom I so loved in life,
I feel myself impelled to sing
again.

Grateful
That he who served
His state and townspeople so well
Was dignified by swift demise,
I sing.

Helen Christopher

He and Mama had together molded a family rich in love and the ability to grow, to learn, to lead useful and fulfilling lives. For the future, Mama chose to remain in the three bedroom house we'd grown up in. But the live-in housekeeper, whom William and I thought she should have, was let go after only a month or two. Mama liked the familiar, and her friends and neighbors did what small town friends and neighbors do to ease the grief and aloneness of one who has lost her partner.

William and I tried to insure that she felt the closeness of our love. We phoned or wrote often. I suggested that she visit our family in Olympia, and perhaps consider a place of her own, where we could keep in contact daily. We all realized that her spirit of independence would preclude her living with the family of either William or me.

Mama made the trip to Olympia in July. It was only to visit; Wilbur was her home. The spring in her step and the sparkle in her eyes seemed sadly diminished. When I entered the guest room to call her for dinner late one afternoon, I found Mama sitting on the side of the bed silently weeping. She looked so vulnerable, so alone.

I put my arms around her. "Oh, Mama," was all I could say.

She answered my unasked question as I held her close. "I miss Will," she whispered. "I miss your father."

🍂

Seven months after Papa's death, Mama's neighbor Cleo Cosby from across the street phoned. It was 5 p.m. Mama had suffered a heart attack.

"But don't tell your mother I called," she pleaded. "She doesn't want you to worry."

I promised and said I'd leave Olympia that night to arrive early the next morning.

Another call came in. It was from another friend of Mama's. "Don't feel you must start tonight," Mrs. Guttschmidt said. "I'm with your mother now and can stay as long as I'm needed."

Then Mama wanted to speak. Shakily she urged me not to start before the next day. I assured her that I wouldn't.

"Goodnight, dear Mama. I'll see you tomorrow—in the afternoon."

At six o'clock the next morning as I was preparing to leave, I answered the phone's ring once again.

Mama was gone.

🍂

In fifty-three years of shared responsibilities and decision making, of joys, of difficulties overcome, Papa and Mama had become a uniquely balanced whole. After Papa's death the balance was gone. And as she quietly let go of life, Mama's heart had simply stopped beating.

"She died with dignity," the doctor said, "Just the way she lived."

That was on September 7, 1957. Mama was ready for the journey that would let her be with Papa once again.

Good-bye to My Twin

Nothing had prepared me for my twin's death of congestive heart failure, five years later, on Sunday, October 14, 1962.

Front page headlines of *The Wilbur Register* announced:

"William Gray, Jr. Dies in New York...He was survived by his wife, Fredrika, at the home in Rye, New York; a daughter, Mrs. Robert Cone of Connecticut; two sons, Lawrence, New York City, and Bruce, at the home; his twin sister, Mrs. Ian Christopher (Helen Gray) of Olympia, Washington; and two granddaughters, Joyce and Karen Cone...

He began his journalistic career under Mr. Barber, editor of The Wilbur Register, during his high school days and rose to the position of assistant managing editor of LIFE Magazine, and as editor of the three international editions, Overseas Edition, Spanish Edition, and Panorama, which is edited and published in Italy."

In the upper right hand corner, next to the masthead was a special editorial:

"The Boy Who Made Good—This is the story of the home town boy who made good. It's a story that's told by every small community, for it seems as if all have developed a particular affection for at least one of their former residents who succeeded beyond the normal in their particular vocation.

"Wilbur's home town boy who made good was William P. Gray, Jr.

" 'Young Bill,' as his father called him, was near the top of his profession when death ended his career this week. As a responsible "Life" and "Time" magazine editor, he was respected by people throughout the world who recognized his importance and ability.

"The Register feels a special tie to the late young Bill since some of his earliest journalistic training was received while working for this newspaper during his school days. We also feel a tie as a friend, knowing how highly he thought of his home town acquaintances. We thoroughly enjoyed his too infrequent visits. We will miss his occasional letters and cards

126

and we will miss having the opportunity to tell everyone about the home town boy who made good."

After my twin's death in 1962, it was written in the Spanish American edition of LIFE that he had served as Foreign Correspondent. The article said:

"William Price Gray was Editor of LIFE's International Editions for twelve years. He brought to this position a wealth of experience as TIME-LIFE Correspondent abroad and as Senior Editor of LIFE. He was a perceptive reporter, an accomplished editor and a kind and gentle man, with a perfect blend of good humor and good judgment.

"Bill Gray became Editor of LIFE's International Editions in 1950. Under his hands these editions flourished and achieved distinction and respect everywhere.

"More than a fine journalist, he was an eloquent spokesman for his magazine and his country.

"His death is mourned by us all. But his legacy to us all is one of which any man, journalist or statesman could be proud."

It was while a storm ravaged our coast that William died. And as he was laid to rest, many mourned. Along with others I wept.

My twin was gone.

To the boy from *Double Entry* who made it big in the world of international journalism, who made his hometown proud to cradle the stone that covers his ashes at the foot of Papa's and Mama's graves in the Wilbur Cemetery—a final good-bye.